Introduction to German Legal Methods

Introduction to German Legal Methods

by

Reinhold Zippelius
EMERITUS PROFESSOR
UNIVERSITY OF ERLANGEN-NÜRNBERG

Translated from the Tenth German
Edition by

Kirk W. Junker
and
P. Matthew Roy

CAROLINA ACADEMIC PRESS
Durham, North Carolina

K
212
.Z56513
2008

The original German 10th edition is published by Verlag C. H. Beck oHG, Munich, © 2006

Library of Congress Cataloging-in-Publication Data

Zippelius, Reinhold, 1928-
 [Juristische Methodenlehre. English]
 Introduction to German legal methods / Reinhold Zippelius ;
English translation, Kirk W. Junker and P. Matthew Roy.
    p. cm. -- (Comparative legal thinking series)
 Translation of the 10th ed., 2006.
 Includes bibliographical references and index.
 ISBN 978-1-59460-539-0 (alk. paper)
 1. Law--Methodology. 2. Law--Interpretation and construction.
3. Law--Philosophy. I. Title. II. Series.

 K212.Z56513 2008
 340'.1--dc22

                                        2008028708

CAROLINA ACADEMIC PRESS
700 Kent Street
Durham, North Carolina 27701
Telephone (919) 489-7486
Fax (919) 493-5668
www.cap-press.com

Printed in the United States of America

03-20-09

Comparative Legal Thinking Series

This series is designed to give students and practitioners of law in the English-speaking world an opportunity to see how their counterparts in other legal systems also learn to "think like a lawyer." Rather than present the legal thinking of other cultures as secondary literature in the third person, this series takes representative, formative and primary works that students in other countries read during their legal education and translates these works for the English language reader. As a result, an English reader from a common law country can attain the unique inside view of the civil law student. We feel that future lawyer skills require more than passing facility with other legal systems through secondary literature, and that this approach of insider comparativism through primary texts is the only acceptable way of knowing the legal minds of one's partners or opponents in international governance, business, and litigation, or of clients' expectations from abroad.

The primary audiences for this book are law students and academics in any English-speaking country, particularly those studying Comparative Law, European Law, Civil Legal Systems, Jurisprudence, or Legal Philosophy. With each translation of primary teaching texts, the English-speaking law student may gain the insight of knowing the way in which his or her counterpart in practice from another country has learned the law. This sort of insight is far more valuable to gaining understanding than the mere information that one acquires either by reading only the translations of the laws themselves or English-speakers' summaries of those laws.

Contents

Foreword   xi

Translators' Note   xiii

Introduction to the English Edition   xv

Works Cited   xvii

Abbreviations   xix

Chapter I   Concept and Function of the Law   3
  § 1. The Law as a Body of Precepts   4
     I.   Duties and Authorizations   4
     II.   The Organization of Authority as the Backbone
           of a Legal Order's Rational Structure   6
     III. Individual Questions   7
  § 2. The Law as "Law in Action"   10
  § 3. The Law as a Solution to Questions of Justice   13
     I.   The Function of a Just Decision   13
     II.   The Standard Gauge of Just Decisions   21
  § 4. Laws as Objectified Regulation   26
     I.   Words as Symbols for Ideas   27
     II.   "Subjective" or "Objective" Interpretation   29
     III. Changes in the Meanings of Laws   34

Chapter II   Structure and Context of Legal Rules   39
  § 5. The Facts of the Case and the Legal Consequence   39

I.   The Relationship between the Facts of the
      Case and the Legal Consequence   39
II.   The Legal Consequence   41
§ 6. "Basic Factual Requisites" and Supplementary
      Provisions   43
§ 7. Conflicts between Legal Norms   50

**Chapter III   Interpreting, Supplementing, and Correcting
                 Statutes**   59
§ 8. The "Classical" Interpretive Criteria   59
§ 9. A Verbal Starting Point, and the Range of a
      Statute's Interpretation   62
I.   "Constructing" the Verbal Starting Point   63
II.   Conventional Linguistic Meaning   64
§ 10. The Argumentative Determination of the
      "Appropriate" Word Meaning   66
I.   Interpretation as a Legitimacy Problem   66
II.   Arguments on the Basis of a Law's Underlying
      Purpose (Teleological Interpretation)   69
III. Contextual Arguments   72
IV.   Arguments of Justice   79
V.   Decision Analyses   81
VI.   The Relationships between Interpretive Arguments   84
VII. Open Questions   86
§ 11. Supplementing and Correcting Statutes   88
I.   Identifying Gaps in the Law   88
II.   Filling Gaps   92
§ 12. Comparing Cases by Type   98
I.   Comparing Cases by Type as a Means of
      Interpretation and Gap-Filling   98
II.   Comparing Cases by Type and Its Interplay with
      Other Arguments   104
III. Honing in on (Specifying) the Legal Consequence
      through Case Comparison by Type   105
§ 13. Effectiveness and Legitimacy of Continued Legal
      Development   107

I.   The Development of Enforceable Law   108
II. The Binding Character of Previous Decisions   110
III. The Legitimacy of Continued Legal Development 112
IV. On the Effectiveness of Legal Development
     Contrary to Existing Rules or Norms   115

Chapter IV   Application of Legal Norms   117
  § 14. Finding the "Relevant" Legal Norm   117
    I.   Methods of "Entry"   117
    II. The Function of the Power of Judgment   121
  § 15. The "Question of Fact"   122
    I.   The Question of Fact and the Question of Law 122
    II. The Establishment of Facts   124
    III. The Judicial Establishment of Facts in Particular 126
  § 16. Subsumption and Room for Interpretation   130
    I.   The Legal Syllogism   130
    II. Substantiation: Interpretation or Subsumption? 131
    III. Justifiable Decisions   134
  § 17. Discretionary Decisions   137

Chapter V   Logical Formalization and Data Processing
            in the Law   145
  § 18. Logical Formalization in the Law   145
    I.   The Notion of a Calculated Law   145
    II. The Limits of Feasibility   146
  § 19. Electronic Data Processing in the Law   150

Index   155

Foreword

Overstatement is a child of fashion. Methods of thought in jurisprudence thus tend either to overstate the rationality of judicial findings and, in particular, the ability of the logical instrument (following the example of conceptual jurisprudence), or to understate them (following the ideals of *Freirechtslehre*). The following treatise seeks to avoid both approaches.

Pursuant to the principles of separation of powers and legal certainty, it follows that the law sets general norms that are binding upon administration and adjudication. Accordingly, administrative and judicial bodies must determine as a matter of principle, and according to rules of interpretation, what the intent of these norms are; and, in so doing, they must abide by that intent. At the same time, however, consideration must also be given to the principle function of the law in providing just solutions to problems. Therefore, statutory interpretation (interpretation of laws) must strive for fair solutions to problems in line with what is linguistically and logically possible (§§ 3Ib, d; 10 IV). The function of the law in offering solutions capable of attaining consensus to questions of justice can also, however, come into conflict with the strict obligation of the law. That happens when the statute, as interpreted according to the rules of the art, apparently does not satisfy its function in serving justice. When, in such a case, the grounds for doing justice outweigh the grounds for separation of powers and legal certainty — which speak for the strict adherence to the wording of the statute — then supplementing or correcting the statute is necessary (§§ 3Ib; 11).

With all this, the limits of methodical effort become clear. Considerations structured according to interpretation and rules of legal development boil down in the end to nothing more than dissoluble values and areas of leeway in decision-making. In short, the interpretation and development of the law are indeed capable of being rationally structured; however they are not completely capable of being rationally determined. (§§ 3 Ib; 10 VII).

This introduction to method is based on the legal science ideas that I set forth in my "*Legal Philosophy*" (4th Edition, 2003). The questions dealt with there are, at the very most, only briefly discussed here; this is particularly so as it relates to the basic concept that legal development is carried out in "experimental thought," in which a continuous attempt is made in finding just and functionally capable solutions to the problems associated with everyday human interaction—solutions which, in an ongoing fashion, are exposed to practical tests and improvements (*id.* at § 11 III).

This treatise also follows the thought, as it relates to its ideas of legitimacy, that the individual whose conscience is governed by reason is the last authority of our sense of justice. On this basis, ideas capable of majority consensus can be obtained and clarified in rational thought. (*id.* at §§ 11 II4; 18 et seq.). Additionally, "legal philosophy" is referred to when it comes to conflicts between law and equity (*id.* at §§ 6; 24) and to some extent systematic and deliberative thought on the solutions of legal problems (*id.* at §§ 38 III; 39).

The beginning student who seeks an initial, general reference pertaining to the steps in which the application of a law to a case is carried out, may begin by reading §§ 6 and 14 of this introduction to method.

I am grateful to Professor Delgado Ocando for bringing this work into the Spanish language. I am also grateful to Dr. Bernhard Schloer and Mr. Roman Kornuta for their translation into Ukrainian. I also wish to once again thank Ms. Brigitte Schulz for her help in proofreading and correction work.

Erlangen, September, 2006
Reinhold Zippelius

Translators' Note

Whenever possible in this text—the first English language translation of Professor Zippelius's treatise—we have relied on previous English translations of German materials when those translations provide the standard for the English version of the German text, or when the translation seemed the most appropriate and authoritative. In particular, when translating sections of the German Civil Code, set forth as examples in the text below, we relied on Simon Goren's translation in *The German Civil Code*, Fred B. Rothman & Co., Littleton, Co (1994). Additionally, when translating specific terms of art or other words and phrases particular to the German legal system, we consulted the excellent translations by Tony Weir of Konrad Zweigert and Hein Kötz's *Introduction to Comparative Law* and Franz Wieacker's *A History of Private Law in Europe*.

German scholarly typography uses different conventions than those of English texts. We have changed most to serve the English language reader. One will find that a few necessarily remain, however. For example, like other German authors, Professor Zippelius uses two different font sizes in the main body of his text. The smaller font is used to provide illustrations, examples or deeper background that should not be relegated to footnotes. Also, literature lists and footnotes in the German version do not provide all the information to which the English-language reader might be accustomed. In some places, we have changed the forms of the citations to look more familiar to the English-language reader, but have neither added nor removed information.

While Hein Kötz himself has remarked that Tony Weir's English translation of the *Introduction to Comparative Law* was superior to the original German, we can only hope to have done justice to Professor Zippelius's fine work.

Pittsburgh, March, 2008

Kirk W. Junker

New York, March, 2008

P. Matthew Roy

Introduction to the English Edition

This book is a translation of Reinhold Zippelius's *Juristische Methodenlehre*, (Munich, C.H. Beck, tenth edition, 2006). The approach of the original German-language volume is to engage an audience of civil (in this case, German) law students with the processes by which one learns the law and reasons in the law, with a special emphasis on the limits and possibilities of one's practice of law based upon that reasoning and those learning methods. As a result, an English reader from a common law country can attain the same unique inside view as that of the civil law student. Thus, to echo the common claim of American legal education when it says that it teaches students to "think like a lawyer," the title of Zippelius's work in English could easily be *Thinking Like a German Lawyer*. We believe that this approach has advantages over works that digest continental-civil law education and summarize it in English. That approach gives one books that are secondary literature whereas the Zippelius text is primary literature. We feel that future lawyer skills require more than passing facility with other legal systems through secondary literature, and that this approach of insider comparativism is the only acceptable way of knowing the legal minds of one's partners in business, opponents in litigation, or clients' expectations from abroad through their primary texts. We chose this volume because of its wide influence in Germany. One can find the original in any German book shop that contains a section for law students. Zippelius has maintained a title in German scholarship that one finds among the nineteenth century works of Friedrich Karl von Savigny (*Juristische Methodenlehre*), and many of the twentieth century German legal scholars who are included in the works cited herein.

Thus the book provides not only intellectual insight in comparative legal systems, but also equips the practitioner with knowing how the civil lawyer sitting across the table understands law. This translation gives the reader an insider's perspective, in a short format, of the same foundation as the civil lawyer himself or herself, rather than either secondary commentary, or an attempt to cover the details of a particular area of law that all-too-soon become out of date. We piloted several chapters of the English translation at Duquesne University School of Law in a Comparative Law of Europe seminar, and the students clearly recognized the opportunity to see how German students are trained, and found the text to be uniquely helpful in understanding theoretical bases for some German legal practices and ways of legal thinking. Given our goal and purpose, we have left Zippelius's examples and citations to German law in the original form, and only translated the law, rather than looking for English or American examples that might generally illustrate the points. The publisher of the original German version has this to say on the cover:

> In order to understand the law, it is essential to understand the methods used in finding the law. Reinhold Zippelius gives us the required knowledge — independent of the philosophical disputes that exist in the law. His treatise seeks to reclaim the law's clarity to the greatest extent possible, while keeping in mind the fundamental task of the law: enabling just solutions to problems.

Works Cited

The works here are cited only by the publisher's name and date of publication. The literature cited before individual paragraphs and sections throughout the book is cited in the same way.

Adomeit, Klaus, Rechtstheorie für Studenten, 3. Aufl. 1990

Bydlinski, Franz, Juristische Methodenlehre und Rechtsbegriff, 2. Aufl. 1991

Demko, Daniela, Zur „Relativität der Rechtsbegriffe" in strafrechtlichen Tatbeständen, 2002

Engisch, Karl, Logische Studien zur Gesetzesanwendung, 3. Aufl. 1963

—Einführung in das juristische Denken, 10. Aufl. 2005, hrsg. und bearb. von Th. Würtenberger und D. Otto

Esser, Josef, Vorverständnis und Methodenwahl in der Rechtsfindung, 2 Aufl. 1972

Fikentscher, Wolfgang, Methoden des Rechts, Bd. III 1976, Bd. IV 1977

Frosini, Vittorio, Gesetzgebung und Auslegung, 1995

Germann, Oskar Adolf, Probleme und Methoden der Rechtsfindung, 2. Aufl. 1967

Heck, Philipp, Das Problem der Rechtsgewinnung und andere Abhandlungen, hrsg. von R. Dubischar, 1968

Höhn, Ernst, Praktische Methodik der Gesetzesauslegung, 1993

Joerden, Jan, Logik im Recht, 2005

Kaufmann, Arthur, Beiträge zur juristischen Hermeneutik, 1984

—Das Verfahren der Rechtsgewinnung, 1999

Kaufmann, Arthur/Hassemer, Winfried/Neumann, Ulfrid (Hrsg.),

Einführung in Rechtsphilosophie und Rechtstheorie der Gegenwart, 7. Aufl. 2004

Kelsen, Hans, Reine Rechtslehre, 2. Aufl. 1960

Koch, Hans-Joachim/Rüßmann, Helmut, Juristische Begründungslehre, 1982

Koller, Peter, Theorie des Rechts, 2. Aufl. 1997

Kramer, Ernst A., Juristische Methodenlehre, 1998

Kriele, Martin, Theorie der Rechtsgewinnung, 2. Aufl. 1976

Larenz, Karl, Methodenlehre der Rechtswissenschaft, 6. Aufl. 1991

Larenz, Karl/Canaris, Claus Wilhelm, Methodenlehre der Rechtswissenschaft, 3. Aufl. 1995

Lege, Joachim, Pragmatismus und Jurisprudenz, 1999

Looschelders, Dirk/Roth, Wolfgang, Juristische Methodik im Prozeß der Rechtsanwendung, 1996

MacCormick, Neil, Legal Reasoning and Legal Theory, 1978

Maschke, Andreas, Gerechtigkeit durch Methode, 1993

Müller, Friedrich, Juristische Methodik, 9. Aufl. 2004

Nawiasky, Hans, Allgemeine Rechtslehre, 2. Aufl. 1948

Ott, Edward E., Die Methode der Rechtsanwendung, 1979

—Juristische Methode in der Sackgasse? 2006

Pawlowski, Hans-Martin, Methodenlehre für Juristen, 3. Aufl. 1999

Raisch, Peter, Juristische Methoden, 1995

Röhl, Klaus F., Allgemeine Rechtslehre, 2. Aufl. 2001

Rüthers, Bernd, Rechtstheoric, 2. Aufl. 2005

Schapp, Jan, Hauptprobleme der juristischen Methodenlehre, 1983

Schmalz, Dieter, Methodenlehre, 4. Aufl. 1998

Schneider, Egon, Logik für Juristen, 5. Aufl. 1999

Schröder, Jan, Recht als Wissenschaft, 2001

Vogel, Joachim, Juristische Methodik, 1998

Wank, Rolf, Die Auslegung von Gesetzen, 2. Aufl. 2001

Weinberger, Ota, Rechtslogik, 2. Aufl. 1989

Winkler, Günther, Theorie und Methode in der Rechtswissenschaft, 1989

Zippelius, Reinhold, Rechtsphilosophie, 4. Aufl. 2003

—Recht und Gerechtigkeit in der offenen Gesellschaft, 2. Aufl. 1996

—Das Wesen des Rechts, 5. Aufl. 1997

—Verhaltenssteuerung durch Recht und kulturelle Leitideen, 2004

Abbreviations

AcP   Archiv für die civilistische Praxis [Archive for Civil Practice]

ARSP   Archiv für Rechts- und Sozialphilosophie [Archive for Legal and Social Philosophy]

BFH   Bundesfinanzhof [Federal Finance Court]

BGB   Bürgerliches Gesetzbuch [Civil Code]

BGH   Bundesgerichtshof [Federal Appeals Court]

BGHSt   Entscheidungen des BGH in Strafsachen [Decisions of the BGH in Criminal Matters]

BGHZ   Entscheidungen des BGH in Zivilsachen [Decision of the BGH in Civil Matters]

BVerfG   Bundesverfassungsgericht [Federal Constitutional Court]

BVerfGE   Entscheidungen des BVerfG [Decisions of the BVerfG]

DÖV   Die öffentliche Verwaltung [Public administration]

DVBl.   Deutsches Verwaltungsblatt [German Administrative Bulletin]

GG   Grundgesetz für die Bundesrepublik Deutschland [Constitution for the Federal Republic of Germany, *literally* "Basic Law for the Federal Republic of Germany"]

JZ   Juristenzeitung [Lawyers' Newspaper]

RGSt   Entscheidungen des Reichsgerichts in Strafsachen [Decisions of the Imperial Court in Criminal Matters]

StGB   Strafgesetzbuch [Penal Code]

StPO   Strafprozessordnung [Rules of Criminal Procedure]

VerwArch   Verwaltungsarchiv [Administrative Archive]

ZRP   Zeitschrift für Rechtspolitik [Journal for Legal Politics]
ZZP   Zeitschrift für Zivilprozess [Journal for Civil Litigation]

Introduction to German Legal Methods

Chapter I

Concept and Function of the Law

The word "method" denotes the path to a goal. In the sciences, a method is a path that leads through rational and therefore comprehensible and controlled means to a theoretical realization, a practical understanding, or even to the boundaries of knowledge.

The subject determines the method. In terms of the law, the questions that the law poses and through which theoretical means seek the answers to these questions, is assessed according to the nature and function of the law.

The law regulates conduct (§ 1). Based on the classical differentiation between theory and practice, this means that legal norms are not intended to help understand the world we live in, but rather serve to order conduct. This means that, in the end, legal norms boil down to practical norms or operating precepts. Therefore, every legal provision contains either precepts providing for a particular action or omission, sections of such precepts (legal definitions), or conditions laying the basis for general or individual duties (authorizations). From a methodological standpoint this is important, for example, for the development of legal norms. These norms, depending on their basic type, contain statements concerning the duties that arise depending on the conditions (§ 5). The question regarding a specific duty to act (payment of compensatory damages or criminal prosecution) and the legal norm that justifies it typically constitute the first steps in solving a legal case (§ 14 I a).

The law is the realized regulation of conduct (§ 2). On the one hand, the law is an organization of conduct that has reliably good chances of being enforced in a standardized proceeding. From a

3

methodological perspective, this aspect is significant for the problem of continued legal development (§ 13 I). On the other hand, the law attains meaning first by way of its application (§§ 14 et seq.); not until it has been applied has it attained its goal.

Laws are rules put into words (statutes). Subsuming laws into words makes statutory law the object of semantic problems and methods that take up a considerable part of the teaching of legal methods. (*See* §§ 4 II, III; 9 II; 10).

The function of legal norms is to resolve legal problems in a just manner (§ 3 I). Methodical thinking is defined by this principle in several respects. This function of the law not only provides important arguments and guidelines for interpretation, (§ 10 IV), but also for the supplementation and correction of laws (§ 11).

§ 1. The Law as a Body of Precepts

I. Duties and Authorizations

Literature: Kelsen, 1960; Nawiasky, 1948; Zippelius, 2003 § 3 (for further information).

The law, as well as custom and moral norms, controls human behavior. This type of behavioral governance differs fundamentally from all other natural control processes, such as those associated, for example, with biology or technology. These fields make use of natural forms of causation that are the subject of theoretical observation. On the other hand, normative controls demand a specific action or omission, which in turn motivate how humans make decisions. The "practical" sciences are concerned with these controls, legal science among them. This difference between theory and practice — or between observation aimed at understanding and the order of conduct — reaches back to the earliest of times.[1]

---

1. *See e.g.* Plato, *The Statesman*, 258; Aristotle, *Metaphysics*, 1025 b; Diogenes Laertius, III, 84.

Following the Kantian distinction between "ought" and "is" statements, neo-Kantian legal philosophy portrayed the law as a body of prescriptions and proscriptions, or "ought" norms.[2] The law does not describe facts, but rather prescribes conduct and results in "prescriptive" statements.

The law therefore consists of obligations to do something or refrain from doing something, as well as rules regulating the creation, modification and termination of behavioral norms or individual rights (or parts of such norms, e.g. legal definitions, *see infra*, at § 1 III).[3] The circumstances and conditions that give rise to behavioral duties are also found, particularly in early legal orders, within the principles relating to the development of customary law. In law found in codes (statutes), the essential conditions for the creation and modification of legal duties are found in the rules relating to regulatory authority (authorizations; institutions possessing legal authority) and regulatory procedure. These determine who may enact general laws or provide the basis for or modify individual duties, as well as the procedure that must be adhered to thereby. An authorization, thus, may be aimed at laying the basis for, modifying, or terminating not only general laws, but also individual legal duties. For example, traffic law authorizes the traffic officer to stop a motorist. The Civil Code (BGB), for example, authorizes laying the basis for certain individual legal rights of the parties by entering into a contract (§ 311, ¶ 1 BGB).

---

2. *See* Zippelius, 2003, § 15.

3. Kelsen, 1960, 57; Nawiasky, 1948, 13, 99 et seq. Deviating from the colloquial use in Germany (*see infra*, at § 2 b), H. L. A. Hart (*The Concept of Law*, 1961, 77 et seq.) characterized "primary norms" as the binding norms and "secondary norms" as the rules (authorizations) which give rise to the prerequisites under which legal duties are justified or modified.

II. The Organization of Authority as the Backbone of a Legal Order's Rational Structure

Literature: M. Jestaedt, *Das mag in der Theorie richtig sein*, 2006, 23 et seq.; Kelsen, 1960, particularly 228 et seq.; Zippelius, 2004, Chs. 7 and 9.

The authorizations that constitute the basis of legally-binding behavioral regulations form a structured body of institutions within an organized (state or supranational) legal community. This structure serves not only the separation of powers principle. Organized authority is also the backbone of a rationally structured legal order. Within this legal order, the various institutional authorities must be arranged and ordered in such a way that the norms and decisions they promulgate contribute to consistent (conflict-free) and well-functioning behavioral organization.

The central organizing formula consists of the "hierarchy of institutional authorities." In the state, the constitution lays the basis for the authority of the legislature; statutes lay the basis for the authority of regulatory bodies; and even duty-creating or duty-modifying individual acts—whether they are judicial decisions, administrative acts or private legal transactions (acts of private autonomy)—require legal authorization. The ranking of rules promulgated by institutional authorities corresponds to the position the authority holds within the hierarchy. Inconsistency within behavioral organization is avoided: Norms that conflict with law that holds higher hierarchical ranking are invalid. Conflicting norms of equal rank strip each other of their validity. And no legally significant individual act may conflict with a legal norm. Administrative acts that conflict with a legal norm are voidable or void ("precedence of law"). Private legal transactions that conflict with a legal norm are invalid.

By authorizing legally binding rules of behavior, institutional authorities create areas of leeway in legal decision making. Even the interpretation of a statute is not strictly determined and leaves open to judicial adjudication the possibility of making certain choices and value assessments (§ 10 VII). Yet, this order of institutional authorities—through its layered hierarchy of authorizations—preserves, step by step, not only the consistency of the law, but it also contains guiding elements and brings order—albeit limited—to its lively, diverse interactions.

III. Individual Questions

The purpose of legal statements is to prescribe an action or omission. However, actual legal statements seem to run contrary to this purpose. For example, Section 223 I of the Penal Code (StGB) reads: "Any person who physically abuses or harms the health of another is punished with imprisonment up to 5 years or a fine." This statement is wholly a statement of fact; the word "ought" or "may" is nowhere to be found. Nevertheless, this norm cannot be understood simply as a mere description of a fact. It does not wish to say that everyone who commits such physical abuse is actually punished, as when the law of gravity instructs that every rock one lifts from the Earth and then releases falls back to the ground. Moreover, this provision seeks to accomplish two things. First, it seeks to prevent two people from hurting each other physically. Second, it seeks to enable the judge to punish persons who violate this provision. This penal measure, therefore, results in two different norms: a "primary" norm, which regulates interpersonal behavior, and a "secondary" sanctioning norm, which directs a legal body—namely, the judge—to react to the violation of the first norm with a penalty. (§ 2).

Quite often, some thought and deliberation is necessary in recognizing certain legal provisions as components of a larger body of behavioral rules or authorizations. Take § 311 I of the Civil Code (BGB), mentioned earlier. It states: "A contract between the parties is necessary in order to create an obligation by legal transaction or to alter the content of an obligation." Here, the conditions are given under which the duties arise, for example, between buyer and seller, landlord and tenant, and employer and employee.

However, these conditions are not fully enumerated in § 311 BGB. The requirements under which an effective legal transaction is effectuated are found in §§ 104 BGB et seq. These sections provide, *inter alia*: "Persons without capacity to enter into a business transaction are 1) those who are under the age of 18; 2) ... ; 3) ..." (§ 104 BGB); and: "declarations of intent from those who are without capacity to enter into a business transaction are invalid." (§ 105 I BGB). Here we are dealing with more remote negative conditions for establishing legal duties.

Some thought, therefore, is often required in identifying certain provisions as components of a body of behavioral rules. Here it becomes clear that the conceptual technique of the law often dissects individual terms or provisions into "legal aphorisms." As such, the individual *fragments* are difficult to recognize as sections of duty-justifying or duty-modifying norms (§ 6).[4]

Now what about provisions that regulate a legal situation "allowing" something? Such precepts either make clear only that certain actions are not at all prohibited or they designate specific prerequisites under which an otherwise valid prohibition is not valid. For instance, it may generally be prohibited to build a house without the appropriate government permit. The regulations pertaining to building permits indicate the prerequisites necessary under which someone is exempt from the general construction prohibitions. Accordingly, it is understood that only the logical structure of the "permit" is set forth; it is not said, for instance, that the construction itself factually constitutes an exception. In fact, this normative scheme (prohibition subject to certain exemptions) serves as a technical instrument, bringing what is fundamentally desired with respect to construction activity into more controlled channels.

The more difficult task is recognizing the normative content of property-based rights, e.g. of possession of a thing. Inherent in such rights, is not a specific state of being or man's dominion over a thing being described? Is possession of a thing capable of being expressed in terms of behavioral precepts? It becomes clear that this is the case when we inquire into the legal relevance of property. This legal relevance exists insofar as members of the legal com-

---

4. *See also* Engisch, 2005, 74, et seq.

munity may not take away, destroy or damage a thing belonging to somebody else. In other words, they are compelled to avoid engaging in certain behavior as it relates to the property owner. After all, rules that regulate the transfer of property are there to denote the criteria under which adjustments or suspensions of certain rules apply in this overall body of duties (§ 5 II). Of course, as it relates to property, the question of whether it is correct that all the institutions of law consistently result in behavioral regulations is one that arises quite notably. For example: Is possession of a dog not primarily a relationship of care and dominion which exists directly over the animal, and secondarily a relationship to other people in that they are prohibited from appropriating the dog for themselves or giving it poisoned meat?

The relationship to things deemed to be in someone's possession is part of everyday life; this is protected and guaranteed by property law. The safeguarding of these various areas of everyday life and interests is important—perhaps plainly even the entire purpose of legal behavioral regulation. But that does not change the fact that it is the norm—commanding an action or omission—that is the legal-technical instrument used to attain these goals. For example, what I claim in court by virtue of possession regarding my garden or my dog always results in the duties of other people, e.g. a duty to pay compensatory damages, replevin, or omission. Even when a mere claim is raised seeking to determine a property right vis-à-vis another person, it is raised for the sake of regulating behavior that arises from the property, and out of which follows, for example, who can prohibit whom from stepping foot upon a certain piece of real property. The provisions relating to property and all other legal rules which regulate a *legal status* (such as power of attorney or legal capacity) do not describe mere states of being, but rather they set forth criteria of practical norms, e.g. organization of human conduct.

Generally, "subjective rights" can be traced back to duties and the power to create duties. Juxtaposed to these rights are the rights of others—for example, the right of a certain price by the seller and the buyer's duty to pay. Moreover, the seller has the power to sue the buyer for payment. On the basis of the right to civil process (secondary norms), the seller can move a court to engage in actions which are directed toward investigating, and if necessary, enforcing the buyer's duty to pay under the Civil Code (primary norms). If, on the other hand, there exists only a legal duty in someone's favor and he cannot enforce his claim in a binding way (one that would oblige a legal body to act), then, though he "benefits," he is not a "beneficiary" in the full legal sense.

§ 2. The Law as "Law in Action"

Literature: J. Binder, *Grundlegung zur Rechtsphilosophie*, 1935, 136 et seq; Th. Geiger, *Vorstudien zu einer Soziologie des Rechts*, 4th ed. (1987) 30 et seq., 90 et seq; R. Pound, *Law in Books and Law in Action*, 44 *American Law Review* 12, 1910; Zippelius, 2003, §§ 4,5 IV.

a)   The purpose of a precept is not to describe what people actually do, but rather to express a requirement not "refutable" through digressive behavior, e.g. by ignoring a traffic signal or "dining and dashing." In sociology, this has been called a "counterfactually stabilized behavior expectation."[1]

The "valid basis of a norm," that is, the reasons why one should follow it, according to Kelsen, can "only be that of another norm."[2] In this sense, one considers the validity of lower norms to be based in higher norms:[3] The basis of regulations is in statutes, and statutes find their basis in the constitution of the state. This regress into higher norms cannot go on forever and, according to Kelsen, ends with only one required norm: One ought to act in accordance with the constitution.[4]

---

1. N. Luhmann, *Rechtssoziologie*, 2d ed. (1983) 43.
2. Kelsen, 1960, 196.
3. Kelsen, at 228 et seq., 239.
4. Kelsen, at 197, 205, 443.

But the validity problem is not yet put to rest. Even if legal norms are not set aside based on individual violations, they have in their *effectiveness* a very real component: The possibility is high that they will be followed and enforced within the legally-constituted community.[5] After a revolution, the pre-revolutionary constitution no longer "is valid" because in reality it is no longer followed, even if the sense and meaning of its norms is still accessible. The new constitution, and law enacted according to it or the law that continues on, "is valid" because it is followed and enforced.

In this sense, customary law, as well as judicial legal interpretation or gap-filling, attain validity to the extent the possibility of their enforcement in a court of law increases (§ 13 I). Guaranteed law shares the characteristic of being an effective and realized order of norms with other "social norms," particularly with the norms of social ethos and custom.[6]

b)   The distinctive feature of the *"guaranteed" law* of the state lies in the specific technique by which it is enforced, namely, that it has a reasonably good chance of being enforced in a *legally-organized enforcement proceeding*. There exists, for example, a good chance that the legal duty of the buyer (in paying the agreed upon price) will be enforced by judgment and execution of a court. Other duties, such as the duty not to kill others, are guaranteed by penal sanctions, i.e. there exists a good chance that the violation of this prohibition will be prosecuted by the district attorney and punished by the various bodies and courts of the criminal justice system. This chance brings with it, more or less, a high degree of probability that such norms will be enforced.

In the legal-technical sense, this norm guarantee functions such that certain *"secondary"* norms supplement the *"primary"* norms

---

5. In a somewhat complicated fashion, Kelsen takes this fact into account when he says: "Effectiveness is anchored as a condition of validity in the basic norm." (1960, 212, 215 et seq.)

6. *See* Zippelius, 2003 §§ 5 III, 6 I, 27 II.

that directly regulate the behavior of members within the legal community. Under more specifically-defined conditions, it obligates legal bodies to enforce those primary norms.[7] The obligations upon these bodies can be sanctioned, for example, by means of a criminal provision against the obstruction of justice or through ministerial provisions. In this manner, the legal order constitutes a "meshed" system of rule, the elements of which—like the patterns of a weave—support and rest on one another. At any point along this organized normative control system the question of course remains open: "*Quis custodiet custodies?*" In a legal system particularly, it may come to pass that certain superior legal guarantee norms never live to see the opportunity to be enforced procedurally, but rather can only hope for the chance to be applied.

Of course it is not necessary that the legal guarantee is always driven by the compulsory rule of law. In fact, voluntary compliance with norms, societal constraints or even the mere threat of procedural enforcement are normally sufficient to allow the legal order to function as a general orientation scheme.

After all, within that specific technique of enforcement lies the characteristic attribute of the guaranteed law of the state. Its uniqueness is intimately connected with the characteristic of the state as an organization equipped with the power of enforcement. As a question of method, the possibility of enforcement is most important for the question of continued legal development. It continually comes to pass that at a particular stage of legal development, certain interpretational possibilities, legal principles or gap-fillers are introduced into the discourse and only gradually attain standing. In other words, the probability grows that they are accepted by the various legal bodies. For example, as it relates to criminal culpability in cases of an impossible attempt, subjective theory has emerged in this very fashion as the pre-

---

7. Nawiasky, 1948, 13, 99 et seq. in connection to A. Thon, *Legal Norms and Subjective Law*, 1878, I § 3. Deviating from the colloquial use in Germany, H. L. A. Hart (*The Concept of Law*, 1961, 77 et seq.) characterized "primary norms" as the binding norms and "secondary norms" as the rules (authorizations) which give rise to the prerequisites under which legal duties are justified or modified (see above § 1 I).

dominate interpretation. The superlegal state of emergency as a criminal liability justification, as well as the positive breach of contract as a civil liability cause of action, also gained standing in this manner (§ 11 II). This means that from a certain stage of legal development onward one could rely on courts applying these particular interpretations, legal justifications, or causes of action (§ 13 I).

However, the concept of the law as a realized control leads onto another methodical trail. In matters of legal application there are questions relating to the reciprocal allocation of norm and concrete case (§ 14 II), the applicability of a norm's interpretation to a case (§ 16 II), and the problem of the subsumption of a particular set of facts under a general norm (§ 16 I).

§ 3. The Law as a Solution to Questions of Justice

I. The Function of a Just Decision

Literature: *See* § 10 IV; Bydlinski, 1991, 317 et. seq; Esser, 1972; *Gnaeus Flavius* (H. Kantorowicz), *Der Kampf um die Rechtswissenschaft*, 1906; H. Isay, *Rechtsnorm und Entscheidung*, 1929, 56 et seq.; M. Kriele, 1976, 167 et seq.; G. Radbruch, *Einführung in die Rechtswissenschaft*, 9th ed. (1952); G. Radbruch, *Vorschule der Rechtsphilosophie*, 1947, §§ 7 et seq.

a)   "*Ius est ars boni et aequi.*" The law is the art of good order and justice. It's no accident that this maxim finds itself at the beginning of the greatest and most influential work of jurisprudence.[1] The law must regulate human behavior in such a way that necessities and encumbrances are distributed equitably, conflicting interests fairly balanced, actions worthy of criminal liability justly punished, and in short, that the legal problems that arise in a society are resolved in a just and equitable manner. Such legal questions take on many forms: Should one be compelled to fulfill the terms of a contract entered into on the basis of malicious fraudu-

---

1. Digests, 1, 1, 1.

lence; should a seller be compelled to take back a faulty product; and if so, in what time frame? What type of punishment should a judge impose on a burglar? What criteria must be fulfilled in order to allow someone to build a house? Moreover, fundamental questions concerning fair social order arise. For example: According to which legal models can compromises be found between the need to freely pursue individual self development; as much uninhibited private initiative as possible; and freely disposable property on the one hand, and the interests of protecting the socially weaker in society and fair distribution of wealth on the other? The answers to these questions ought to be as fair and just as possible. At any rate, we raise this demand, even in light of the fact that a particular statute, several statutes, or judicial decision does not comply with our demand, and the legal question cannot be solved justly.

In addition to the task of doing justice, there are the requirements of legal certainty, and optimally and adequately satisfying competing interests. These goals demand their consideration when interpreting and supplementing legal provisions (§ 10 I). They stand in a complex relationship; they can complement or run contrary to each other. As such, the law undisputedly serves, appropriately and optimally, to satisfy societal interests. However, this is not simply attendant to the interests present in the society, but rather that the law should create a just order of these interests.[2] The general composition of legal norms aims at legal certainty, and by inhibiting arbitrary unequal treatment, justice as well. On the other hand, by neglecting the particularities of an individual case, the law can run contrary to the demand for justice.[3] Justice and legal certainty come into conflict in questions concerning the legal effect of a materially-incorrect judicial decision. In this case, depending on the circumstances, greater weight can be ascribed to legal certainty or to justice.[4] There are, after all, legal norms which only serve the func-

---

2. Zippelius, 2003, § 9 III.
3. Zippelius, 2003, § 24.
4. BVerfGE 3, 237.

tion of giving order but do not substantively decide a question of justice, e.g. traffic regulations according to which the right lane is a travel lane and the left lane is for passing. With these qualifications however, one can thus be sure that the purpose of the law lies in bringing about just solutions to the problems that arise between people.

This notion is demonstrated in the early history of jurisprudence: in Salomonic judgments, in kadi jurisprudence, but chiefly in case law such as in the *ius honorarium* of Roman praetorian law and in Anglo-Saxon "case law," as practiced to this day. Here, concrete cases sought a just solution and provided the direct impetus for a judicial decision. The general legal principles deriving from these decisions thus have their roots in the duty to provide just solutions to social conflicts.[5] However, legal arrangements with codified law have a component of *judge-made law* as well, particularly as it relates to judicial legal development. This component develops and makes the law more precise in areas where the hermeneutic instrument has left the choice between several interpretative alternatives open, or where legal provisions have gaps that need to be filled (§§ 10 et seq.). Similarly, the *common law*—developed through legal cases—serves the function of solving legal problems in a just manner. As common law, therefore, an injunction is enforced only when, in the prevailing opinion of those living within the legally-constituted community (the *opinio iuris* of the legal community), it appears as the equitably-acceptable ordering of particular circumstances. Only under these criteria will the binding character of a rule gain acceptance in the community (*opinio necessitatis*).

Today, as societal relations are regulated largely through legislation, questions of justice arise predominantly in this area. When not denigrated to arbitrariness, legislation seeks to create a just behavioral order that sensibly weighs the interests of community participants against one another. Legislation, too, creates legal norms

---

5. Zippelius, 2003, § 18 II.

principally while endeavoring to find just solutions to problems inherent in the coexistence of human beings. This principle determination does not foreclose the fact that there may be value-indifferent legal norms that simply fulfill a function of order. Nor does it rule out the possibility that legal norms are from time to time in reality the effluence of imprudent or unjust legislation.

b)   Several *conclusions for the legal method* result as concerns the function of law in arriving at fair, interest-preserving and compatible solutions to legal problems.

First of all, the following caveat is to be noted: Inasmuch as the legislature has decided legal questions and the substance of the legal issue presented can unambiguously be determined through the means of interpretation, those applying the law are bound fundamentally by the solution to the problem and decisional criteria determined by the legislature as applicable to the legal issue at hand (§§ 11 Ic; 13 III). Accordingly, even questions of justice are predetermined by the legislature. The restriction of one's self to dogma in the service of the application of the law corresponds to the principle of separation of powers and, at the same time, serves the interests of equal protection and legal certainty.

Legal terms regularly have an area of play or leeway with regard to their meaning (§§ 4 I; 9 II). The hazy area that goes along with many of these meanings can be narrowed down methodically through interpretation, but this often does not clear up the haze. Interpretation is not an exact method; rather it boils down, for the most part, to a decision between several interpretive principles and possibilities present in the discourse. This decision is legitimately affected by a choice among the remaining interpretative alternatives that lead to the most just solution (§ 10 IV). This function of legal interpretation—justly finding a solution to the legal question at hand—can already be seen influencing the understanding of individual legal words.[6] Examples of this include the different mean-

---

6. Zippelius, 2003, § 39 III.

ings associated with the word "negligent," as it relates to criminal and tort law. These differences are justified in that the criminal law and the law of obligations, respectively, deal with different questions. For example, §§ 223 et seq. of the Penal Code (StGB) sets forth the circumstances under which injury inflicted upon another is to be penalized under the law. On the other hand, § 823 I BGB controls as it relates to when those very circumstances call for just compensatory damages. This correlation to certain legal problems[7] leads to different interpretations of the word "negligent," as it is found in § 229 StGB and § 823 I BGB. (*See also* § 10 III a). In the law of obligations, it is sufficient that the necessary standard of care in a traffic situation is disregarded (objective concept of negligence). For such negligence to be punished criminally, however, it is necessary that the actor was also personally capable of maintaining the standard of care (subjective concept of negligence).

The fact that legal norms are instruments that bring order to daily life does not affect only their interpretation. When these norms, despite all efforts at interpretation, fail to reach a just solution that satisfies a certain sense of the law, it appears to us to be in need of supplementation. Either we ask for this supplementation *de lege ferenda* (through future legislation), or we determine *de lege lata* (pursuant to existing law) that there is a "gap" in the law to be filled by a judge (§§ 11). As such, the function of the law in finding just solutions to legal problems does not merely guide interpretation, but also becomes the touchstone consideration when it concerns the necessity to supplement statutes.[8]

The legal-technical and hermeneutic instrumentalities assist in solving legal problems in a just way, free of contradiction, and protective of interests. Anecdotally, this is seen in the story of the famous Bartolus, who first made his decision then had his friend search for the corresponding *Corpus-Juris*. A legal finding made in

---

7. *See also* R. Wank, *Die Juristische Begriffsbildung*, 1985, 110 et seq.
8. In agreement with the BVerfGE 34, 287.

such a fashion is not guided by arbitrariness, but rather the pursuit of justice and fairness.[9] Radbruch applied these thoughts to interpretive instruments: "Thus, the interpretation is the end, its outcome; the interpretive means are only chosen after the outcome is determined. In reality, the so-called interpretive means only serve to justify, from the text after the fact, that, which in inventive supplementation was already found; and whatever this inventive supplementation may be, there is always one interpretive means or another, one conclusion or counter-conclusion in the offing, ready to justify the decision."[10] In other words, a judge confronted with a particular case already develops a preconception about how to rule according to his own sense of the law. This guides the interpretation of the statute he uses to justify his decision. Josef Esser has breathed new life into this line of thinking.[11] And Goethe's sarcasm resonates: "In interpretation, be spirited and fresh; if you don't interpret it, embellish it."[12]

The idea that legal-technical instruments merely serve an assisting function resonates in the thesis of Philipp Hecks: that there is an "equivalence of construction," that is, the same thought can be expressed in various forms.[13] This equivalence of construction is particularly palpable in the area of comparative law where it has long since been discovered that different legal orders, while they approach the same issues with rather different methods and concepts, often arrive at similar answers.[14] The degree to which the conceptual instruments are involved in problem solving should therefore not be overestimated.

c)   The degree to which the conceptual instruments are involved in problem solving, however, should also not be underestimated.

---

9. Kantorowicz, 1906, 21, 46.
10. Radbruch, 1952, 161.
11. Esser, 1972. *Cf.* Looschelders/Roth, 1996, 71 et seq.
12. J. W. Goethe, *Zahme Xenien* II.
13. Ph. Heck, *Begriffsbildung und Interessenjurisprudenz*, 1932, § 16.
14. E. Rabel, in: *25 Jahre Kaiser-Wilhem-Gesellschaft*, vol. 3, 1937, 91.

Rational structuring of legal considerations — the legal concept which is brought into the solution of a problem — serves to clarify, narrow, and often times correct rough ideas of what the right result is. Even the solution to legal problems occurs in concert with preliminary judgments and the subsequent understood usage with its conceptual structures.[15]

As such, *interpretive criteria* (§§ 8, 10), for example, serve to guide the discussion vis-à-vis the argumentation. The interpretive criteria, namely, give problem-solving a conceptual layout such that it can be conceptually structured. In this manner, the criteria function as *key concepts* in the treatment of a legal problem without solving it themselves fully (§ 10 VII).[16]

In similar fashion, general legal principles (§ 10 IIIc), particularly proportionality, prohibition against excess, and the principle of equal treatment all serve the function of approaching a problem conceptually, bringing it into conceptual terms capable of discussion without, however, offering a definitive solution. This is the case, for example, when the legislative body decides on an issue of social benefits and must find a compromise between the principles of the social state and frugal budgeting; or when the legislature considers regulating the criteria under which a declaration of intent can be challenged, the principle of private autonomy on the one hand, and confidentiality in legal transactions are to be taken into consideration.

---

15. Zippelius, 1997, Chs. 8 and 9.

16. The function of concepts and principles in serving as instruments, which guide the discussion of argumentation as factors involved in resolutions or as "Topoi," have been described for jurisprudence most notably by Viehweg and Perelman. (Th. Viehweg, *Topik und Jurisprudenz*, 5th ed. (1974) §§ 3, 8; Ch. Perelman, *Juristische Logik als Argumentationslehre*, 1979, §§ 58 et seq.) As to the concept of "key concepts," which make problems approachable: R. Zippelius, *Wertungsprobleme im System der Grundrechte*, 1962, 22, 82; E. Denninger, "Verfassungsrechtliche Schlüsselbegriffe", in: *Festschrift f. R. Wasserman*, 1985, 288 et seq.

The important thing in these cases is finding the right manner and measure, appropriate to the situation at hand, under which one of these principles can be asserted. Here, the measure according to which competing principles and the interests and freedoms represented by these principles are to be realized, acts in accordance with the principle of proportionality and the prohibition against immoderation, both of which help legal considerations further conceptually produce (§ 10 V).

In such general legal principles, guiding ideas, significant in a particular legal culture in providing solutions to legal problems, are singled out in a more or less pure form. These guiding ideas, therefore, have in normative thought a similar, comprehension-guiding function such as in the one they perform in the area of empirical social research — Max Weber's ideal type — in unlocking the understanding of concrete circumstances of a case.[17] One can also speak of legal principles as "orienting," which as general "perspectives of the legal world" guide one's reflection concerning the appropriateness of a decision.[18] In a discussion of justice these principles also serve as key concepts which do not provide any definitive solutions.

A particularly important rational model of consideration that legal thinking employs is the principle of *equal treatment*. This principle demands that equals essentially be treated equally and unequals unequally. Here, the conceptual framework begins to single out the common and differentiating characteristics of factual findings that have been compared. Then one must ask whether the differences justify or even demand differential treatment, a question which always arises in consideration of a particular problem of justice (§ 12 I b). Even this rational model of consideration does not lead to exact solutions and regularly leaves decisional leeway.

---

17. *See* R. Zippelius, *Allgemeine Staatslehre*, 14th ed. (2003) § 2 III 2.

18. F. Kaulbach, *Experiment, Perspektive und Urteilskraft bei der Rechtserkenntnis*, ARSP, 1989, 455.

d)   Understandably, there can be no dispute that all these conceptual considerations are aimed primarily towards the goal of a just result (§ 10 IV). Kant viewed our thinking as occurring with the guidance of preliminary judgments that give direction and purpose to the use of reason. "Preliminary judgments are necessary, if not indispensable for the use of reason in intensive thought and investigation. These preliminary judgments serve to guide the mind in its inquiries, and to supply it with various means. When we think intensively about a particular subject, we must always make preliminary judgments and nearly already sense the realization which comes to us through this thought." Such preliminary judgments could be called "anticipations," "because one already anticipates his judgment of a thing before he has the dispositive part."[19]

II. The Standard Gauge of Just Decisions

Literature: Zippelius, 2003, §§ 11 II; 18 et seq.; Zippelius, 2004, Ch. 4.

Methodological deliberations lead quickly to the question of what could serve as a standard gauge for an equitable solution to a problem. Seeking the broadest possible intersubjective foundation is the way to decide questions of fairness and justice—namely, as many foundations as possible within the particular legal sentiment, and as many as possible within the notions of justice capable of majority consensus that are based on those sentiments. This opinion has been justified in more detail elsewhere. Here, only the following thoughts are reiterated in summary fashion.

a)   In an "open society," all the "heteronomes," authoritatively-specified natural laws and other ethical "truths," have become questionable. Here, the individual conscience appears as the last moral authority, an authority that the undertaking of ethical insight can expand towards. Thus the open society must search for the basis of

---

19. I. Kant, *Logik*, 1800, 115.

legitimacy that its equitable decisions entail within its members' independent conscience. Everyone appears here to be a moral authority to be regarded equally with respect to others. In questions of justice, the conscience of the individual, the "what I think is right," comes to the surface in his rationally-guided (*see infra at* c) *sense of the law.*

A just community order that is effective for many can only then be reached on the basis of these criteria when it is possible in questions of justice to overcome subjectivity, and, through free and open debate, come to a general, or *at least* majority consensus. Indeed, it has been shown that consensus is possible regarding values. For example, when several people find behavior tactless, a rescue selfless and brave, or the penalty imposed on another cruel, they are then opining, from case to case, to have substantively understood something the same. The same applies when they find it unjust when cases that are not substantially different are not treated equally. Thus, we assume that, as they do upon us, certain events impart upon other people values of like qualitative substance. Certainly this is not strictly provable, just as little as the fact that other people can look at a "green" field and pick up the same impression of the color. The fact that both things are the case is simply part of the self-evident, but in the strictest sense, improvable hypotheses upon which our daily life is based. This view in no way implies an invariant, unalterable, and absolute "empire of values," which are fixed on a hierarchy. But here one finds the contention that different people can arrive at substantive ideas, capable of achieving consensus, which are based upon substantively coinciding values (§ 4 I).

b)   Our values tend to diverge when we must balance various goals and interests. This is particularly the case when it comes to those questions of justice that play an important role in community life. Here, individual predispositions and environmentally-influenced preferential tendencies assert themselves as qualifying factors. These balancing questions engender, at most, an agreement only among a fragment of those within the legally-constituted community. In any event, even here a broad basis of common (intersubjective co-incidental) values is often found. The idea is that what matters in legal decisions is not the highly personal view of an individual judge, but rather *notions of justice capable of majority consensus*—this thought had its most memorable manifestation perhaps in the Germanic trial, in which the recommended judgment required the acceptance (Vollbort) of those assembled in the Thing.

For reasons of *practical legitimacy*—notwithstanding the question whether there are moral "truths"[20]—it must follow that questions of justice are decided according to concepts of justice that are capable of majority consensus, rather than very individual ideas and concepts. The *democratic notion* inherently stands for the proposition that as many people as possible should be able to participate in the model of order, and that the judge, as representative of the community, should follow the prevalent beliefs within the community. The principal of *equal treatment* also demands that in cases of the same type, judges, rather than using standards which are dependent upon a particular judge, apply the same standards to their evaluations, these standards being identifiable and enjoying broad consensus in the community. Ultimately, the principal of *legal certainty* demands that the overwhelmingly recognized pattern of conduct and procedures in legal transactions may be adhered to, and that judges respect this in their evaluation.

c)   *Concepts of justice capable of majority consensus* remain a difficult standard. In particular, they may not be flatly equated with what is ostensibly the opinion of the majority. These concepts are often determined by various interests rather than through conscience, a manipulated sort of bandwagon mentality, rather than independent judgment. Therefore, the challenge arises in guiding consensus-building onto paths of considering questions of justice rationally.

----

20. *See* Zippelius, 1996, Ch. 10.

After the free exchange and airing of arguments, the decisions must be made in a justified and rationally structured (1c) manner that is capable of review. When decisions are made on the basis of laws, i.e. according to general rules prescribed prior to the case to be decided, this serves to provide some distance between a one-sided commitment to an interest on the one side, and the rationality of a decision, on the other.[21] Even otherwise, decisions must be made in accordance with the rule of law. In this respect, decision-making authorities that approach conflicts neutrally and competently are necessary.

In a representative democracy, just decisions are sought vicariously through representation for the people as a whole. It is the legitimate duty of these representatives and, moreover, high courts to help guide how the public forms its views of the law, and to guide these views into rational paths of argumentation. According to the democratic understanding of legitimacy, however, such a duty only serves to clarify what is capable of achieving majority consensus. In other words, finding decisions that will stand up to the particular sense of the law of most people and which are fit for acceptance by the majority.

Just like the jurists of yesterday, the actors of today's representative democracy must also be capable of reaching acceptable decisions (requirement of *acceptance*). Toward that end, they do not see themselves pressed only by the guiding image of democratic legitimacy, but by a very real pressure for legitimacy. If the people's representatives amass decisions that the majority finds unjust or unreasonable, they lose both democratic 'authority' and, in the long run, the opportunity to be effective.[22]

The institutional and procedural means of a constitutional state with separation of powers cannot guarantee that questions of jus-

---

21. *See* Zippelius, 1997, Ch. 11 c.
22. Zippelius, 2003, §§ 11 II 4; 20 III, IV; 21 I.

tice are decided solely on the basis of the legal consciousness of the majority and not on the basis of personal interest or manipulated views. But, on the whole, these means improve the chances that these decisions come closer to this guiding image.

d)   The question still remains how one makes the very indeterminate gauge of "notions of justice capable of majority consensus" palpable and "operational" for those charged with applying the law. In German proceedings, for every concrete legal decision, one could obtain acceptance of the overwhelming portion of the (male) legal community. In larger and more complicated polities such as the modern state, one must consult other manifestations of the prevalent social, and in particular, moral law. For jurisprudence, the ideas of justice and fairness that are accepted in the community in mature law find their most important written expression above all in the value judgments of the constitution. This expression is based upon the assumption that, at least in the grand scheme of legal development, such ideas of equality capable of consensus in the community permeate and are maintained. Both in the legal-ethical relevant legal norms and in the legal principles developed administratively and by case law, we find a "legal-ethical context" to the individual legal problems (§ 10 III c). Here we have the manifest characteristic of a legal-ethical tradition which has developed step by step while continuously orienting itself to other comparable solutions to problems. Moreover, indications of the social morale of a legal community can also be found in the areas of tradition or common usage and the growing institutions of social life (§ 10 IV).

Even where legal decisions develop the law and go beyond what has already been determined, the ability to attain consensus is desired to a high degree. Only decisions capable of attaining consensus can expect to be accepted by those living within the legal community without substantial opposition. In this manner, that which is capable of attaining consensus builds tradition; in turn the tradition of attaining consensus lends backing and support to concrete legal findings. Similar ideas are found in Anglo-American legal thought. It has been said of Anglo-American judges that they seek support in "common sense" and in the consensus of the public as it relates to social values.[23]

To the extent the statute allows the judge a certain amount of decision-making ability as it relates to what is just and fair (I b), and to the extent the particular value decisions of the statute and other indicators fail to offer a reliable basis for the notions of justice that are capable of consensus, the decision must rely on the judge's personal sense of the law in all its relativity. Even a judge's personal sense of the law does not supply a sure answer to some questions of justice. Every jurist knows such "borderline cases," situations of legal-ethical perplexity, situations in which decisions can only be obtained in a legal-ethical venture. These are situations in which justice is not found, but rather is ventured and created in a draft. So also the judge encounters issues where he has lost the clarity of the law and the sure and doubt-free guidance provided by the rules of interpretation and the principles of fairness and justice. Justice is, after all, not simply a pure process of understanding, which to its fullest extent, is determined in advance through objective criteria. It is on these boundaries—the ostensibly assured constancy of a legal and social-ethical order that challenge the personal sense of the law and the venture of justice—where we see that jurisprudence plays a role in the vitality of the common arrangement. Where decision-making leeway is left to the judge in interpretation and gap-filling, the judge can influence the development of the law. In this manner, legal application, too, becomes a moving moment of development in which guaranteed law and legal morale are consistently found.

§ 4. Laws as Objectified Regulation

Literature: N. Hartmann, *Das Problem des geistigen Seins*, 1932, Ch. 44 et seq.; J. Kohler, *Lehrbuch des Bürgerlichen Rechts I*, 1906, 122 et seq.; G. Schwalm,

---

23. MacCormick, 1978, 149, 236.

Der objektivierte Wille des Gesetzgebers, in: *Festschrift für E. Heinitz*, 1972, 47 et seq.

I. Words as Symbols for Ideas

Literature: D. Busse, *Juristische Semantik*, 1993; J. Hruschka, *Das Verstehen von Rechtstexten*, 1972, 27 et seq.; W. Kamlah / P. Lorenzen, *Logische Propädeutik*, 2nd ed. (1973) 27 et seq.; F. v. Kutschera, *Sprachphilosophie*, 1971, 117 et seq.; J. Lyons, *Einführung in die moderne Linguistick*, 1971, 409 et seq.

Laws (statutes) set legal ideas into words. Vesting these ideas into words makes them communicable and gives them a fixed form that also serves the interest of legal certainty. The law can keep itself within the channels of the already prevalent social morale. In this case, notions of approved behavior that are accepted by all, or the majority of those within a community of laws, become legally binding even before their codifications were treated as guides to behavior. The law, however, can also distance itself from these ideas, e.g. in a dictatorship, and in extreme cases the law can be the offshoot of a tyrannical lawmaker.

For now, we shall postpone asking whose ideas are decisive (the lawmaker, the plurality of those within a legal community, etc). First, it is necessary to consider the way in which ideas are at all "objectified" through spoken or written words, that is, how they can be expressed through readable or audible symbols. How is it, for example, that a pair of lines which may look foreign to us can evoke the image of a horse in the mind of a Korean, or that the marks "red rose," which are neither red nor take on the form of a flower, can evoke the image in our minds of a red flower? Because they have been memorized as symbols that stand for sounds, which in turn stand for certain objects that the symbols "denote" and which are practiced into memory. In as much as words serve as symbols for the expression of experiences, they are exemplarily, i.e. by way of example, introduced and practiced. This happens from childhood on when a word is spoken indicating a particular thing or occasion: "That is a rose"; "that is a horse"; "it's thundering."[1] Once the association is established, a sym-

---

1. *See* Kamlah/Lorenzen, 1973, 27 et seq.

bol with which one has learned to connect the experience calls it into memory. Like father and son, teacher and student, this is the manner in which people within a linguistic community learn to associate the same symbols with the same substantive experiences. Once this is done, someone may use the symbol (word) which has been introduced to represent a particular experience in order to arouse an idea with the same content in another person. The same applies to certain senses where intersubjective understanding is possible, i.e. commands and logical statutes. When it comes to the meaning of a word, we understand here certain expressions of ideas (expressions of experience or sense) which the word signifies and "suggests."

Ideas "conveyed" by words (e.g. Little Red Riding Hood, the wolf, or a mathematical theorem) can be communicated to others (transsubjective) as expressions of ideas which can be repeatedly invoked in our memory (or which are able to be combined from elements presently in memory). They can be juxtaposed (obicere) to the mental processes in which they become "current," and are in this sense "objective."[2] Words denote certain experiences or senses reproducible in the imagination and "suggest" them. The "substantive meaning" of a word can also be characterized as the "concept," which is connected with the word. In this sense Kant described the (general) concept as, "a general notion or an idea of something common to several objects."[3] Word and concept are therefore to be distinguished. This is demonstrated by virtue of the fact that different words sometimes refer to the same concept (the same general substantive idea). The words "contract" and "*pactum*" mean the same thing.

The universal every day "concepts" of people, things and occurrences we also describe as "types." Hence, we are not following the common and rigorous partition of concept and type. Both terms denote "that common thing, passively preconstituted, perceived within the cloak of the individual and on the basis of this cloak the emanating "one," "identical."[4] "Concepts" of the sort mentioned, i.e. the concept of the small child, mountain or pine tree, refer to, as one takes

---

2. Zippelius, 2003, §2 II 2.
3. I. Kant, *Logik*, 1800, §1; *see also* Husserl (n. 4).
4. E. Husserl, *Erfahrung und Urteil*, 1939, §81.

it as the "type," an arrangement of characteristics rather than a mere sum of characteristics. In addition, however, there are concepts that do not reflect the "arrangement of characteristics" of visible objects, that is, they do not portray "types." Examples of this are "abstract" concepts of individual markers or characteristics, for example: "red" and the terms for numbers. The question of whether and in what sense that "identical universal" has an ideal being is for another discussion.[5]

Understanding a statute means ascribing to the words of the statute a general idea connected with them. It is not rare, however, for the text of a statute to be ambiguous, that is, the text is capable of being identified with several different ideas or notions (more on this in § 9 II). For example, there could be several ideas of when a "person" exists in terms of Art. I of the Constitution (GG), a person could exist at conception, implanting of the egg, at a particular fetal developmental stage, or at birth. Differing ideas with respect to this question are *a fortiori* connected with value concepts. This can be seen when people differ on what it means for something to be "immoral," or what exactly constitutes "gross negligence." As it relates to the words in a statute, there is often flexibility and play when it comes to their meaning. Circumscribing the meaning of a statute is the main task of legal interpretation.

II. "Subjective" or "Objective" Interpretation

Literature: E. R. Bierling, *Juristische Prinzipienlehre*, vol. IV, 1911, 197 et seq., 230 et seq., 256 et seq.; Engisch, 1997, 106 et seq.; Fikentscher, 1976, 662 et seq.; Germann, 1967, 66 et seq., 378 et seq.; G. Hassold, "Wille des Gesetzgebers oder objektiver Sinn des Gesetzes," in *ZZP*, 94 (1981) 192 et seq.; Larenz, 1991, 32 et seq., 301 et seq.; Looschelders/Roth, 1996, 29 et seq.; A. Mennicken, *Das Ziel der Gesetzesauslegung*, 1970; Nawiasky, 1948, 126 et seq.; G. Radbruch, *Rechtsphilosophie*, 8th ed. (1973) § 15; F. C. v. Savigny, *System des heutigen Römischen Rechts*, I, 1840; U. Schroth, *Theorie und Praxis subjektiver Auslegung im Strafrecht*, 1983; H. Wuestendoerfer, "Zur Hermeneutik der soziologischen Rechtsfindungstheorie," *Archiv für Rechts- und Wirtschaftsphilosophie* 9, 1915/16, 304 et seq.

a)   Words stand for certain ideas or notions to which the words refer and which the words denote and awaken associatively. When

---

5. Husserl (*supra*), § 82 n. 3.

someone uses a word, he often connects with it a somewhat different imagined content (sense) than the recipient; and from that one can differentiate the sense connected with it by members of a particular group of persons. Words can therefore be ambiguous. This means, in particular, that the imagined content that various people connect with one and the same word may more or less strongly deviate from one another. In other words, different people have different ranges of idea or perception in which the same word can be appreciated differently by each person. When it comes to imagined content that is connected with value statements, such as "immoral," highly personal opinions come into play. The question then becomes: "From which of the respective ranges should the meaning be taken?" The question relating to which range of ideas is controlling plays an apparent and important role (§ 10 II). We are confronted here, however, with a general problem of semantics that consequently is dealt with in several fundamental aspects. The debate over the subjective and so-called objective theory of interpretation arises from the issue described here. The subjective theory of interpretation operates on the assumption that statutes are binding statements that have their basis in the will of those who took part in the legislative process. Thus, in its most pointed form, the subjective theory takes the view that the interpretation should be as close as possible to the personal notions of those taking part in the passing of the legislation.

The objective theory, on the other hand, takes the view in its most pointed form that it is not the intention of the legislator which is to be investigated, but rather the intention of the statute itself. Statutes, however, are always the expression of human ideas. Therefore, the proper meaning of the text is to be ascertained from people's range of perceptions, even if one regards it as impossible or undesirable to go back to the highly personal notions of those who participated in the legislation's passage. Instead of such an approach, one could consult the wide breadth of ideas, i.e. legal and political policy goals or understandings of justice which are common to a plurality of people, about which an intersubjective understanding can occur, and which in this sense are "objective."[6] However, here we are presented with the difficult question of which of these substantive ideas is decisive: Are they the ideas accepted by a majority of those within the legally-constituted community or the ideas prevalent among the elites? Additionally, it is not easy to grasp and make operational the social norms capable of attaining consensus in a community (§ 3 IId). A further question to be asked is: Which purposive ideas or notions of justice should be ascertained, those at the time of the statute's passage or those at the time of applying the statute?

As the literary historian will attest, not only jurists are confronted with problems of interpretation; anyone who endeavors to understand the words of another encounters such problems. When the literary historian writes a biographical study about a poet, he tries from the poet's poems to extract those ideas that the poet connects to his poems. In this case, "subjective interpretation" is being undertaken. But even a poem lends itself to readings with other purposes in mind. For example, one can inquire into which prevalent notions of the time it gives expression to, or which general understandings conceal themselves in the various potential meanings of the word, even if the poet himself was not conscious of all of them. It is also the task of a poem and a poet to encourage such ideas. This is what Geibel meant when he said: "A good poet has hardly done his job if one cannot read more into his works than that which he originally intended to put in." Here it becomes clear that the choice between subjective and "objective" interpretation is influenced by what the interpreter is interested in doing.

b)   Thus the jurist asks which of the various possible meanings should interest him. If he thinks it is correct to obediently implement the will of a tyrannical dictator, then he will seek out the "will of the leader" by means of subjective interpretation.

---

6. Zippelius, 2003, § 20 I.

On the other hand, objective interpretation seeks notions that are familiar to the mindset of a wide number of people. Consequently, to attain such an interpretation, one would have to approach it from the perspective of the Historical School, which saw the law a product of the *Volksgeist*.[7] Yet Savigny did not account for this unmistakably enough and is thus considered it to be "subjectivist." When, in his words, the interpreter "should place himself into the thoughts of the legislator and seek to simulate or recreate his activities," then he is not recreating highly personal thoughts, but rather those that the legislator must have thought as representative of the *Volksgeist*. (*See infra* § 8).

One must approach an objective interpretation from the standpoint, for example, of Hegel's philosophy, as well. According to this philosophy, the history of the world is a process in which objective reason unfolds. This would manifest itself in the *Geist*, e.g. the laws and customs of the people. Within this process, legislators and courts would have to be mere medians.[8] Based on this, interpretation would have to strive for selecting the most reasonably objective semantic meaning of a statute. This is related to the view that the organized power internalizes and relies on the living "objective *Geist*" and gives it consciousness, initiative and the ability to act.[9] Statutes would then be "objectifications" of that objective *Geist*. As such, the interpreter would have to seek the meanings of words that correspond best to the prevalent and living ideas within the community.[10]

One could therefore also say that the interpretation one chooses depends upon the type of philosophy of the state one has. Even the few examples here demonstrate that interpretation theory is not always a simple choice between the "subjective" and the "objective"

---

7. Savigny, 1840, 13 et seq.
8. *See* G. W. F. Hegel, *Enzyklopädie*, 1830, §§ 548 et seq.
9. N. Hartmann, 1932, Ch. 35 b.
10. *See* Hartmann, 1932, Ch. 44c, 57, 58 b.

interpretation, but that many varieties of interpretation theory are conceivable with different components of "subjective" and "objective" factors.

c)   In a representative democracy with a system of separation of powers, it is assumed that the members of the legislative body are responsible for the division of functions in the state and elect through its statutes certain ends—legally binding—and a method for their realization. Even here, the statute is based on a decision made by certain people in order to achieve certain ends. Subjective interpretation theory in its sharpest form, described *supra,* fails already practically by virtue of the fact that the personal ideas of those members of the legislature voting in favor of a particular law are hardly in harmony with each other and are difficult to ascertain. The motives expressed in legislation, and those typically formulated in the ministries, cannot be flatly assigned to those who made the legislative decision. Moreover, under a democratic understanding of legitimacy it would not be permissible to simply rely on the personal views of members of parliament. Even in a representative democracy there is an element of direct democracy: Even if the representative bodies need not follow each and every sway of public sentiment, they must legitimately orient themselves towards the notions of justice capable of consensus as seen by the majority, and they are to give these notions expression in their laws. Even if they wanted to stray from these notions in favor of their own personal ideas, they may not legitimately do it. Consequently, in a representative democracy, the decisions made by the legislature concerning purpose and goals are to be interpreted in line with how the legislature thought about them, or was likely to have thought about them as the representative of the community's notions of what could obtain consensus. Even as such, those applying the law work under the guise of legitimate representation (§ 10 II, IV).

The justification for binding representatives lies in the considerations already discussed (§ 3 II). In an "open society," the notions of justice held by every citizen are held principally in the same regard in relation to one other. For that reason, the open society seeks a basis of legitimacy for its decisions of justice in the notions held by the citizenry—albeit clarified in accordance with the rule of law—which in an open competition of opinions find the widest possible consensus.[11] Inquiring into the notions of justice that are capable of finding majority consensus is aimed at determining which decisions are in harmony with the obtainable understanding of justice of most people—a difficult problem that is not simply resolved by a superficial sampling of daily public opinion. Rather, a "clarification" of such an ability to form consensus is necessary. In a representative democracy based on the rule of law, institutional and procedural provisions should lead to decisions that, as it relates to their conscience and sense of the law, most people can accept (§ 3 II c).

III. Changes in the Meanings of Laws

Literature: Engisch, 2005, 115 et seq.; Germann, 1967, 75 et seq.; Ott, 2006, 54 et seq.; B. Rüthers, *Die Wende-Experten*, 1995; Wank, 2001, §§ 3 II4; 5V; Th. Würtenberger, *Zeitgeist und Recht*, 2nd ed. (1991) 174 et seq.; Th. Würtenberger, "Rechtsprechung und sich wandelndes Rechtsbewußtsein," in: W. Hoppe et al., eds., *Rechtsprechungslehre*, 1992, 545 et seq.

Up to this point, the problem of ascertaining a statute's meaning has only been considered as it relates to the point in time of its passage. Next, the question is placed in an historical and developmental perspective: Legal norms can usually be interpreted within a range of meanings; within such ranges, various meanings can be attributed to the norms. Among these different word meanings, one of them is to be chosen as the interpretation. Along with considering other interpretive criteria, this choice should come as close as possible to the notions of justice most capable of attaining consensus (§ 10 IV). This is in line with the democratic understanding of legitimacy (II c). These notions of justice, however, are capable of changing over time. Thus the question has arisen whether one proceeds according to the notions and ideas controlling at the time the law was passed (interpretation at the time of inception), or according to those that are prevalent today (living interpretation). If one were to follow the latter, then a *change in meaning* of the statute occurs within the range of meaning attributable to the statute's text.

The following considerations speak in favor of a living interpretation: The basis of legitimacy of law to be applied today does not lie in the past; it lies in the present. Today's legal community has access

---

11. Zippelius, 2003, §§ 11 II 4; 21 I.

at any time to the traditional body of law that is now superseded; it can abrogate and amend it or follow the thoughts of Thomas Hobbes,[12] which can be formulated as follows: For the present, it does not matter under whose authority the statute was enacted, but rather under whose authority it lives on today; this also means the notions of justice it would represent if it were enacted today. When, however, the legitimate basis of continuing law lies in the present, then it is also correct to interpret the statute *ex nunc*, i.e. to select the interpretation that comes as close as possible to the prevalent notions.

This is clearly the case when interpreting indefinite legal concepts such as the concept of "contrary to public policy" (immoral). This refers to the historically changing views regarding what is deemed proper with respect to the interactions of the people and through which the content of those actions change.[13] For example, social practices and prevailing social-ethical notions that define the cohabitation of the sexes have changed; these changes have provoked a discussion concerning whether, and to what extent, the constitutional protection of the "family" (Art. 6 Abs. 1 GG) should be extended to arrangements outside of traditional marriage.[14] Even the duties an employer has "in good faith" (§ 242 BGB) in relation to the employee has changed. If, for example, a crane operator on the job negligently damages a loading vehicle and the owner of the vehicle demands compensatory damages in tort (*unerlaubter Handlung*) (§ 823 I BGB), it was earlier understood that the crane operator carried the risk of his hazardous work. Later, social state notions prevailed: These held that according to the doctrine of "good faith," the employer shields the employee in such cases partially or completely from a cause of action for compensatory damages as it relates to third parties.[15]

The change in meaning of a law here may not only be initiated though a change in the prevalent social-ethical notions, but also through changes in actual affairs. Such a change in the actual ways of life can influence the prevalent notions of justice, and through this, indirectly influence legal interpretation.[16] It can, however, also

---

12. Th. Hobbes, *Leviathan*, Ch. 26.

13. BVerfGE 7, 215.

14. *See* R. Zippelius, "Verfassungsgarantie und sozialer Wandel," *DÖV*, 1986, 809, 810.

15. *See* W. Zoellner, K. G. Loritz, *Arbeitsrecht*, 5th ed. (1998) § 19 II 2.

16. Zippelius, 2003, § 12 III.

guide interpretation in other ways: Legal norms must always be substantiated in consideration of the existing realities of life, that is, the subject matter in its specific form and the question of its ability to be subsumed provide the impetus for considering and honing in on a legal norm's range of meaning in light of the subject matter (§ 16 II). In this manner, the development of legal concepts can be caused by the fact that "in their area, new, unpredicted factual patterns arise."[17] As such, for example, new forms of social security were able to influence the interpretation of Art. 14 of the GG,[18] and new communication technologies were able to have an effect on the interpretation of Art. 5 I of the GG.[19]

Of course, interpretive considerations must also bear in mind other interpretive criteria, not the least of which is the separation of legislative and executive power. For this reason, a change in meaning must not only keep itself within the possible meanings of the text of a legal norm, but also, where possible, within that very range of meaning that the purpose of the legislation leaves open for honing in on. The longer the period between the initial passage and subsequent application of the legal norm, however, the greater the freedom is to develop the law. Moreover, the longer the period, the stronger the necessary contemplation of changing social-ethical notions thrusts aside the requirement of realizing unchanged the original purpose of the statute. "The interpretation of a legal norm cannot always remain faithful in perpetuity to the meaning ascribed to it at the time of its inception. One must consider the reasonable function the norm plays at the time of its application. The norm constantly resides within the context of social conditions and societal or political views that the norm should influence. With these views, its content should and must change under certain conditions. This is particularly the case when legal views and ways of life have so fundamentally changed between the adop-

---

17. BVerfGE 2, 401.
18. BVerfGE 53, 290, 291.
19. BVerfGE 57, 322, 323.

tion of a norm and its application—as has been the case [in the twentieth] century."[20]

The interpretation of legal norms is also determined in part by changes in culture-shaping ideas.[21] However, not every change in thought or popular opinion justifies assuming that there has been a change in a law's meaning. Under a democratic understanding of the prevailing Zeitgeist, a legitimate basis of interpretation only exists when it is identified as a development of the notions of justice that flow from the majority through a process of a search for consensus guided by reason (§ 3 II c).[22]

---

20. BVerfGE, 34, 288, 289.
21. Rüthers, 1995; Würtenberger, 1991; Zippelius, 2004, Ch. 1 II.
22. Zippelius, 1997, Ch. 8, 11 c, d.

Chapter II

Structure and
Context of Legal Rules

§ 5. The Facts of the Case and the
Legal Consequence

Literature: Engisch, 2005, 12 et seq.; Larenz, 1991, 250 et seq.; N. Luhmann, *Rechtssoziologie*, 2nd ed. (1983); Nawiasky, 1948, § 17; A.v. Tuhr, *Der Allegemeine Teil des Deutschen Bürgerlichen Rechts*, II 1, 1914, § 43.

I. The Relationship between the Facts of the
Case and the Legal Consequence

Legal norms usually provide that certain obligations (legal consequences) arise, are dispensed with, or are modified under certain criteria—namely, upon the occurrence of a specific set of facts. For example, Section 823 I of the BGB states: "A person who willfully or negligently injures the life, body, health, freedom, property or other right of another unlawfully is bound to compensate him for any damage arising therefrom." Pursuant to § 823, therefore, a person shall do something (compensate another person), when certain conditions occur (when the person willfully or negligently injures another unlawfully).

The legal norm here contains a qualified command, or, in other words, a "conditional program."[1] This tying-together of the facts

---

1. Luhmann, 1983, 88, 227 et seq.

of the case and the normative legal consequence is a particularly important type of legal norm. There are, however, unqualified legal precepts as well. Penal provisions usually contain an unqualified proscription of behavior to which a penalty attaches — at the most constricted by a "negative condition" that there is no justification. A penal sanction, addressed to the legal decision-making body (secondary norm), attaches to what oftentimes is only an impliedly expressed proscription (the primary norm). This is only the case in a qualified manner, namely, when the factual elements of the offense have taken place.

"Purposive programs" are also not structured according to a scheme of qualified legal consequence directives.[2] These include norms that require an organ of the state to fulfill certain aims or goals without the occurrence of any particular set of facts or other criteria. For example, Section 1 of the Construction Code (*Baugesetzbuch*) requires local communities to come up with construction plans, and in so doing, comport with the goals of well-ordered, environmentally-friendly, and socially-just community construction development. In the area of constitutional law, constitutional mandates and state objectives, such as the principle of the social state, can be described as purposive programs for the legislature.[3]

The following considerations shall focus on conditional legal norms, namely, those that are structured: If ... (set of facts), then ... (legal consequence). The occurrence of a particular set of facts triggers command of particular behavior. The nature of this relationship has been pondered, as well as whether the relationship can be referred to as a legal causality. To be sure, we do not mean causality in the natural sciences sense; the law does not describe natural processes, but prescribes something upon the occurrence of certain conditions. The actual occurrence of these conditions provides a sufficient justification for the existence of the intended legal obligation. This relationship is wholly different from the relationship between a natural cause and its actual effect.

---

2. Luhmann, 1983, 88, 232, 241.
3. Zippelius/Th. Würtenberger, *Deutsches Staatsrecht*, 31st ed. (2005) §§ 5 4III 3b, c; 17 I 2 c.

Nevertheless, when one speaks of "legal causality" and "legal effect," one may not draw impermissible analogies between natural causality and "legal causality" on the basis of similar linguistic usage.

In the normative area, a "legal effect" may be sufficiently justified in several ways. For example, if a taxi driver carelessly runs into something and causes the passenger to break his glasses, the passenger may have a claim for compensatory damages in tort (*Schadensersatz aus unerlaubter Handlung*) (§ 823 I BGB), and also under the terms of his transport contract with the taxi driver. The taxi company is thus liable to pay damages on two bases. Of course, a conflict of norms problem lurks behind such a self-evident statement. This is particularly the case when there are differences in the legal consequence, even if it is only the statute of limitations (§ 7 b). Legal consequences are not only capable of finding multiple bases to justify them, but several co-existing bases may hinder the fulfillment of a legal consequence. A rental contract, for example, which is void as against public policy (§ 138 I BGB) may also be void due to the incapacity of one of the parties (§§ 104, 105 BGB). This means that there are two independent bases for concluding that the contract does not create any legal obligations. However, a contract already retroactively nullified can no longer be effectively cancelled. This is because the cancellation terminates the legal obligations arising out of the rental contract, i.e. proceeds under the assumption that up to the point of cancellation, legal obligations existed. In this case, the basis for nullifying the contract in the first place conceptually precludes the application of any contract cancellation provisions.

II. The Legal Consequence

The law regulates human behavior (acts and omissions) through "should" or "ought" norms. Thus, in the end, legal provisions result in the justification, nullification, or modification of legal obligations (§ 1). General or individual legal obligations arise, therefore, when a proximate legal consequence attaches to a particular set of facts. For example, a statute enabling the enactment of local ordi-

nances designates the criteria under which a local swimming prohibition or street cleaning regulation can be enacted. Section 311
I BGB, already mentioned, provides that under the criteria mentioned therein individual legal liability arises.

The legal consequence may also dispense with certain obligations or relocate them within the obligational structure. For example, contractually-based obligations (the obligations arising from
a sales contract) can be dispensed with by rescinding the contract.
Furthermore, pursuant to certain cancellation provisions, individual obligations arising from a rental contract, work contract,
etc., may be put aside in the future. The legal consequence of other
types of provisions is the waiver from a particular proscription; an
example of this was the construction permit (§ 1 II). The assignment
of a claim means that a new creditor takes the place of the previous one. Even the legal consequence of a conveyance is a reloca-
tion within the obligational structure: Through ownership of a
thing, we know who is prohibited from using the thing and who is
allowed to use the thing at his or her will (§ 1 II). When ownership
is transferred to another, the previous owner is obliged from that
point forward to refrain from use of the thing; the new owner then
acquires the freedom of disposition over the thing.

But not all legal provisions directly tie a normative legal consequence to a set of facts. Sometimes they merely complete obliga-
tion-justifying or obligation-modifying norms as non-independent
supplements, e.g. as legal definitions or exceptions. For example,
§§ 104 and 105 BGB merely provide the conditional exceptions that
preclude the legal justification or modification of individual legal
obligations (§ 1 II).

§ 6. "Basic Factual Requisites" and Supplementary Provisions

Literature: J. Esser, *Wert und Bedeutung der Rechtsfiktionen*, 2nd ed. (1969); Fikentscher, 1976, 654; Larzen, 1991, 257 et seq.; Wank, 2001, § 2.

In the practical cases confronting the jurist, there often are several possible legal consequences. After a traffic accident, the prosecutor is interested in whether any of the participants can be penalized criminally. The civil question arises as to whether one of the participants is liable to another to pay damages. Legal deliberation begins by finding one or more legal norms that demand a legal consequence, e.g. prosecution or civil compensatory damages. Solving the case is substantially a process of examining whether the factual circumstances are such that a crime can be prosecuted or civil liability imposed.

Formulated generally: Within the basic type of legal norm, the abstract set of factual circumstances (FC) is tied to a legal consequence (LC). The prosecutor or attorney interested in pursuing legal consequence LC must then examine whether the factual circumstances FC have occurred. This set of factual circumstances is comprised of a number of individual factual attributes ($f_1 + f_2 + f_3 \dots$) the occurrence of which is to be tested in turn. If all of the individual factual attributes are present, then the legal consequence exists. However, if one of the attributes is absent, the legal consequence does not attach.

a)   The necessary requisites of a legal consequence must often be taken from a number of individual provisions and joined together. The complete factual attributes to be applied to a case must be "constructed" from a "basic set of factual requisites" and supplementary (defining and completing) provisions. The particular norm from which the desired legal consequence arises functions as the basic set of factual requisites (§ 14 I a). The following case is illustrative because it delves into the structure of these constructive relationships: the case's branch-like structure.

Imagine a man of advanced years bicycling through an intersection when, suddenly, he collides with Mr. Fox, who has the right-of-way, is crossing legally, and happens to have just shot a rabbit for himself while out hunting. As a result of the collision, the rabbit slips from Mr. Fox's grip, falls to the ground, and is crushed by oncoming traffic. Fox demands compensatory damages from the bicyclist. The aging bicyclist protests he is not liable; that in an unexpected bout of dizziness he was unable to maintain the usual level of care and, because of this, collided with Mr. Fox.

In solving this case, it is necessary to turn first to § 823 I BGB. This section ties the desired legal consequence (compensatory damages) to a set of factual circumstances which is under consideration in the instant case (injury to property of another): "A person who willfully or negligently injures the life, body, health, freedom, property or other right of another unlawfully is bound to compensate him for any damage arising therefrom."

The damaged thing must be the "property" of another person. Whether this factual attribute of § 823 BGB is present can only be determined with the help of other provisions. Section 958 I BGB provides: "A person who takes into his proprietary possession an abandoned, movable thing, acquires ownership of the thing." Section 960 I 1 BGB adds: "Wild animals are ownerless [abandoned] as long as they are free." The rabbit was therefore to be considered a movable, abandoned thing (§§ 90, 90a BGB) before Mr. Fox shot him. The concept of possession is defined in § 872 BGB: "A person who possesses a thing as belonging to him is [the owner thereof]." Fox appropriated the rabbit to his individual use. The appropriation of the property was also not excluded on the basis of § 958 II BGB. Therefore, Fox acquired ownership over the rabbit according to § 958 BGB.

The bicyclist caused the loss of the rabbit and therefore "injured" the property of another.

The injury must also occur "unlawfully." Conduct which proximately causes injury, i.e. conduct sufficiently related to a legally recognizable injury to be held the cause of that injury, is, in principle, unlawful where there is no defense or justification for such conduct. Such defenses or justifications include: self defense, collective self-defense, self-help, and aggressive state of emergency. These defenses constitute a set of factual circumstances which raise an exception and are considered along with the other factual circumstances required by § 823 I BGB. None of these enumerated defenses or justifications, however, is applicable in this case.

The injury must have resulted from "willful" or "negligent" conduct. The concept of negligence is stated more precisely in § 276 II BGB: "A person acts negligently if he fails to exercise ordinary care." The necessary inquiry, therefore, is the standard of care that was objectively necessary, not whether the bicyclist was physically capable of meeting this standard. The requisite objective standard of care was not met in this case.

The legal consequence must also be specified more precisely, namely, whether compensation is in kind (*in natura*) or monetary. The answer to this question is found in § 249 BGB. Under § 249, the injured person has a choice: Instead of demanding compensation in kind, he may demand monetary compensation when, as in this case, damage or destruction of a thing calls for such compensation.

In this illustration of a simple solution to a case, the starting point was the basic set of factual circumstances necessary to fulfill the legal consequence. It was necessary here to connect particular factual attributes to the desired legal consequence. This case demonstrates that in order to complete the the requisite set of factual attributes, and therefore the necessary legal consequence, resort to further provisions is oftentimes necessary. Not until the totality of the precept is ascertained (the "basic set of factual requisites" along with the supplementary provisions that attach to them) do we have the complete norm to be applied in the instant case. In other words, the provisions taken together contain the sum of all the individual

factual attributes to which the desired legal consequence attaches—
and the requisite specification of the legal consequence itself.

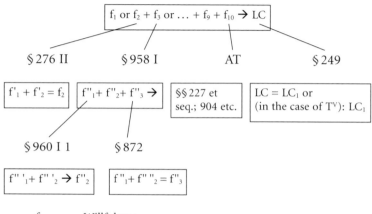

§ 823 I BGB

$$f_1 \text{ or } f_2 + f_3 \text{ or } \ldots + f_9 + f_{10} \rightarrow LC$$

§ 276 II   § 958 I   AT   § 249

$f'_1 + f'_2 = f_2$ | $f''_1 + f''_2 + f''_3 \rightarrow$ | §§ 227 et seq.; 904 etc. | LC = LC$_1$ or (in the case of T^V): LC$_1$

§ 960 I 1   § 872

$f'''_1 + f'''_2 \rightarrow f''_2$ | $f''''_1 + f''''_2 = f''_3$

f_1	=	Willfulness
f_2	=	Negligence
f_3	=	Property (of another person)
f_9	=	Injury to this interest
f_{10}	=	Unlawfulness
$f'_1 + f'_2$	=	Failure to maintain the necessary standard of care in traffic
f''_1	=	Movable thing
f''_2	=	"Ownerless" or abandoned attribute of a thing
f''_3	=	Possession
f'''_1	=	Wild animal
f'''_2	=	Located in the wild (free)
f''''_1	=	A thing
f''''_2	=	Taken into possession as belonging to the person
LC	=	Duty to compensate
LC$_1$	=	Duty to compensate "in kind"
LC$_2$	=	Duty to compensate monetarily
T^V	=	Injury to a person or damage to a thing

The factual attributes that comprise the prerequisites of the desired legal consequence were analyzed in legal memorandum style:
The individual requisites (and their own requisites) were sampled
sequentially. After determining that each of the requisites was satisfied (and at least one of the requisites was satisfied when there

was a choice among alternatives), we could conclude that a legal consequence arose. Had one of these requisites not been fulfilled, or an applicable justification or defense existed, then the legal consequence would have failed to obtain. An analysis of the factual attributes does not follow simply the sequence of the legal text, but the logic of the matter (*Sachlogik*) — for example, the question of whether a protected interest was injured; whether this injury was unlawful, and based on all of this, whether the person causing the injury is liable.

Once a result is reached, the solution to the case can be presented in the "style of a judgment." In so doing, everything necessary to reach a legal consequence which is considered unproblematic is only mentioned briefly. The structure of the presentation could look as follows: Fox may demand monetary compensation or a rabbit of the same value (§§ 823 I, 249 BGB) because: The bicyclist caused the loss of the rabbit (f_9); Fox had ownership of the rabbit (f_3) since the rabbit was acquired pursuant to § 958 I BGB, the rabbit being a movable (f''_1) abandoned thing (f''_2, §§ 90, 90a BGB) and the rabbit was a wild animal ($f''\,'_1$) located in the wild ($f''\,'_2$, § 960 I 1 BGB); Fox appropriated it for his own use (f''_3) and as belonging solely to him ($f''\,''_1 + f''\,''_2$, § 872 BGB); as a licensed hunter he was authorized to make such a capture (§ 958 II BGB); the injury to the property was unlawful (f_{10}); and the injury occurred negligently (f_2) because a person acts negligently when, objectively considered, he fails to maintain the necessary standard of care in traffic ($f'_1 + f'_2$, § 276 II BGB), as was the case here with the bicyclist. (Practically, acquisition of ownership of a thing is only analyzed when ownership is challenged, § 1006 I BGB).

b)   Determining which norm in a concrete case provides the "requisite set of factual circumstances" (starting point) and which legal provisions are "supplementary provisions" depends on the desired legal consequence. For the case just discussed, § 823 BGB provides the starting point because we were interested in the duty of compensation contained in that section. The existence of such a duty to compensate, however, could be just a preliminary question in other cases. Consider, for example, when a buyer wants to offset the seller's requested price with his demand for compensatory damages arising out of § 823 BGB.

The supplementary legal provisions stand in various differing theoretical contexts to the "requisite set of factual circumstances."

In our example from § 823 I BGB, the factual attribute "negligent" is more precisely defined in another provision (§ 276 II BGB). The word "negligent" is thus translated into a compound expression, that is, this expression is considered to bear the same meaning as the original word. Indirectly then, the attributes of § 276 II BGB become part of the set of factual requisites of § 823 I BGB.

Another factual attribute (property of another) is not only defined by a supplementary provision (§ 958 I BGB), but the provision sets forth the criteria necessary to attain ownership of the rabbit. On the one hand, ownership of a thing is the "legal consequence of § 958 BGB. On the other hand, it is a factual attribute pertaining to § 823 I BGB. In this legal-technical manner, the law makes the prerequisites for acquisition of ownership indirectly part of the set of factual requisites of § 823 I BGB.

The factual attribute "unlawful" means that the legal consequence only attaches when no valid justification or defense applies: In particular, none of the exceptions contained in §§ 227 et seq., and 904 BGB (self defense, defensive and aggressive exigency, self help) apply. In this manner, the attributes of these exceptions are thought of and included as "negative factual attributes" under § 823 I BGB.

Finally, § 249 BGB does not supplement the legal factual requisites of § 823 I BGB, but more narrowly specifies its legal consequence, i.e. it further defines the nature and substance of the obligation to compensate.

There also exists the possibility that the legal consequence of another provision may be referred to in its entirety. For example: Section 823 II 1 BGB provides: "The same obligation is placed upon a person who violates a law intended for the protection of others."

Under certain circumstances, a referral is made completely to the legal consequence of § 823 I BGB. Logically, the same result is reached as if § 823 II 1 BGB were to read: "A person who violates a law intended for the protection of others is obligated to compensate that person for any damages resulting therefrom."

When a reference is made to the norm of another statute, a "dynamic" or "static" reference is intended. A dynamic reference occurs where the supplementary norm, with its substantive content, is invoked to complete the referring norm (observing, of course, later textual changes). A static reference occurs when the supplementary norm is continually there, with the substantive content it had at a particular point in time—normally the point in time when the reference norm became effective—completing the reference norm. Ascertaining which of the two references is intended can be accomplished by interpreting the reference norm, in particular by looking at its purpose and the history of its development.[1]

c)   A widely used legal technique to refer to the legal consequence of another norm is the *Fiction*.[2] It is said there was once a provision that stated the following:

§ 1:   The public pool shall be divided into an area for men and an area for women.

§ 2:   Only women may enter the area designated for women.

§ 3:   The pool custodian (*Bademeister*) is a woman for the purposes of § 2.

Section 3 here leads to the same regulation as if the sentence read: "The pool custodian may also enter the area designated for women." Section 2 could also have been formulated to read sim-

---

1. BVerfGE 47, 311; 60, 155; 64, 214; *See* F. Ossenbühl, *Freiheit—Verantwortung—Kompetenz*, 1994, 33 et seq.

2. A subtler observation sees in the fiction not only a reference technique, but an instrument of comparative thought, which can serve—in a targeted selective manner—to pick out important differences or commonalities. Zippelius, 2003, § 18 II; G. Mitsopoulos, *Le Problème de la fiction juridique*, 2001.

ply: "Only women and the pool custodian may enter the area designated for women." Through this fiction, according to which f_2 is tantamount to f_1, the legal consequences that attach to the set of facts labeled f_1 also attach to the deviating set of facts labeled f_2.

This design is the same for more complicated fictions. For example, Section 455 BGB provides: "The acceptance [and thus formation of a binding sales contract] of the purchase of a thing received on a trial basis shall only be valid if manifested within the agreed-upon timeframe. If the thing was handed over to the buyer on a trial basis, his silence is considered acceptance." Here, the legal consequence of the acceptance, i.e. the formation of a binding sales contract under §§ 454 I 2, 158 I BGB, is connected to two sets of facts: (1) acceptance manifested within the agreed-upon time frame, and (2) (alternatively) handing over of the thing to the buyer on a trial basis and his silence within the agreed-upon timeframe. The law in this case expresses the following: A purchase on a trial basis becomes valid when the buyer either accepts the sale within the agreed upon timeframe (T1), or when the thing is handed over to him on a trial basis and he keeps it for the agreed-upon timeframe saying nothing. (T2).

A fiction can also be employed to effectuate an exception. For example, §§ 2 and 3 of the pool provision above could be changed to read:

§ 2:   Men are prohibited from entering the area designated for women.

§ 3:   The pool custodian is not a man for the purposes of § 2.

In this case, § 3 leads to the same regulation as the sentence: "This prohibition does not apply to the pool custodian."

Additionally, one should note that occasionally a differentiation is made between fictions in the more narrow sense and absolute presumptions. A fiction exists where the fictional set of factual requisites surely does not exist (the pool custodian is certainly not a woman). On the other hand, we speak of absolute presumptions when there is the possibility that the "fictitious" set of factual circumstances actually exists; in the case where the presumption does not apply, such a provision indeed does function as a fiction in the actual sense.

§ 7. Conflicts between Legal Norms

Literature: O. Bachof, *Verfassungswidrige Verfassungsnormen?*, 1951; Engisch, 1997, 209 et seq.; D. Heckmann, *Geltungskraft und Geltungsverlust von Rechts-*

normen, 1997, 138 et seq.; A. Klein, *Konkurrenz und Auslegung*, 1997; Larenz, 1991, 266 et seq.; Nawiasky, 1948, 91 et seq.; Ott, 1979, 192 et seq.; Wank, 2001, § 13.

If norms regulating behavior are to provide legal tranquility and a guarantee of helping the citizen orient his or her behavior, then they may not contradict one other; in fact, they must complement one another. If one is to characterize a relationship of individual elements—ordered in such a way as to be free of conflict—as a "system," then legal norms ought to make up a system of behavioral controls that represents an ordering of human coexistence capable of functioning.

The authority to set rules (competencies) serves the "unity of the law." In order for rule-making functions to mesh free of conflict, there is a hierarchy within the organized state: a "layering" of institutional authorities. Statutes can only validly be enacted on the basis of the constitution and the limits set therein; regulations can only validly be enacted pursuant to a statute and according to the limits set by the statute.

But conflicts between the enacted norms themselves are to be avoided. Rules relating to conflicts of norms serve this purpose. A conflict of norms exists when several norms, by virtue of the text of the norms, relate to the same subject matter. In such cases, several solutions are possible: It may be possible to apply both norms concurrently (Examples *see infra*, b); or one norm may make another norm invalid as it relates to the particular area of conflict. In the latter case, the "displaced" norm remains out of force after being neutralized by the conflicting norm (Examples e, f). Finally, it is possible that one norm merely precludes *application* of another norm in the area of conflict: In this case, the "displaced" norm, after being neutralized by the conflicting norm, remains otherwise fully applicable. (Examples c, d).

a)   The following example represents simply an *apparent* conflict of norms because, as will be seen, the code expressly avoids the apparent conflict: A doctor has been called as a witness in court and is to testify regarding facts confided to her by a patient. As a basic principle, criminal procedure requires that anyone who is called to testify before a tribunal in fact appears and testifies (§§ 51, 79 Rules of Criminal Procedure (StPO)). On the other hand, § 203 I of the Penal Code (StGB) prohibits a doctor from revealing, without consent, information confided to him in his capacity as a doctor. The doctor cannot fulfill both duties. However, the law itself avoids a conflict of its own commands: The witness is excused from testimony where he is under a duty of confidentiality, thereby avoiding a conflict of separate duties (§ 53 I Nr. 3 StPO).

b)   When several legal norms in a particular area bring about legal consequences that are in harmony with one another, these norms can often be applied in a parallel manner (cumulative conflict of norms). As seen in the taxi cab example *supra*, the taxi driver is obligated to compensate the passenger on two bases: on the grounds of breach of contract, and tort. In some cases, however, there is considerable reason to seek the legal consequence of only one of the applicable norms.

This applies, for example, as it relates to the claim a lessor (landlord) can raise against a lessee (renter) due to an alteration or deterioration of the rented thing [property]. As a rule, not only do the factual requisites exist that satisfy a breach of contract claim, but the factual requisites also exist to make out a claim in tort (§ 823 BGB). However, resorting to a claim in tort, which has a three-year statute of limitations, would disrupt the purpose of the shorter statute of limitations of a claim in contract (§ 548 I BGB: [Wear and tear brought about by stipulated use] A lessee is not responsible for alterations or deteriorations of the leased thing which are brought about by the stipulated use.)[1] Further, a claim in contract must be based on intent or *diligentia quam in suis*. For example, in gratuitous bailment cases the purpose of reducing liability may not be disrupted independently of the contract claim by allowing a claim in tort for which only negligence is necessary.[2] (§ 690 BGB [Liability in case of gratuitous deposit (bailment)] If the custody is undertaken gratuitously, the depositary (bailee) shall be responsible only for such care as he is accustomed to exercise in his own affairs.)

---

1. *See* BGHZ 66, 319.
2. *See* BGHZ 55, 396.

The decision favoring a cumulative conflict of norms is often based on subtle interpretive considerations. Examined closely, the problem is one of overlapping sets of factual requisites, to which we shall return shortly.

Several norms may be applicable in a given situation, particularly when several compatible legal consequences arise from them. For example, when an official forges an official document in order to defraud someone in a legal transaction, the official meets the factual requisites of both Document Forgery (§ 267 StGB) and the factual requisites for a disciplinary procedure (according to the relevant disciplinary rules). He can be both criminally punished and removed from service under the disciplinary rules.

c)   It is often easy to recognize that out of several norms, all of which are applicable to the factual situation at hand, only one is to be invoked. This is the case usually as it relates to general and special rules. For example, when a fellow stabs his opponent in the arm during a bar room brawl, two provisions apply to the situation based on their respective texts: Sections 223 I and 224 StGB. The former states: "A person who injures the body or health of another shall be imprisoned for up to five years, or shall pay a fine." The latter states: "A person who brings about bodily harm: (1) by poison or other substance hazardous to the health, (2) with a weapon or other dangerous implement, (3) by means of insidious aggression or assault, (4) as a co-conspirator, or (5) through actions that are life-threatening, shall be serve a term of imprisonment of not less than six months and up to ten years. The second provision, therefore, adds further factual requisites to § 223 and provides another legal consequence in the form of a sentencing guideline. Both provisions can be sketched as follows (including intent, § 15 StGB):

$$\S 223 \text{ StGB: } F_1+F_2+F_3 \text{ (or } F_4) \rightarrow LC_1$$
$$\S 224 \text{ StGB: } F_1+F_2+F_3 \text{ (or } F_4) + F_5 \text{ (or } F_6+F_7 \text{ or } \dots) \rightarrow LC_2$$

The factual attributes of § 224 relate to those of § 223 as the more specific concept to the more general. The more specific contains all the attributes of the more general and at least one more con-

ceptual attribute. In this case of "Speciality," the factual requisites
of both competing norms are fulfilled, however it is sufficiently
clear that the legal consequence of the more specific provision
should be applied: *Lex specialis derogate legi generali.* The more
general norm is not to be applied to the types of cases subject to this
special rule.

However, conflicts of norm problems are not always so easily solved. Even
in the case of Speciality there is need for more subtle considerations in order
to answer the conflicts problem. For example, certain ancillary consequences
may attach to the more general norm, e.g. *Massregeln der Besserung und
Sicherung*, (General Laws of Reformation and Security)* which are not fully
encompassed by and are not compatible with the legal consequence named in
the special provision, e.g. a simple penal provision. These ancillary consequences are then possibly applicable alongside the legal consequence of the
more specific provision.

d)   The solution to a conflict of norms problem is particularly
difficult when several statutory sets of factual requisites relate to
each other like two circles overlapping, rather than the narrower-
to-broader relationship. In this case, the conflict of norms problem
cannot be solved according to the principle of logical speciality, but
oftentimes only with the assistance of teleological considerations.[3]

e)   Conflict of norms rules also arise according to a norm's hierarchical status. Higher level law—that which has been enacted
by a higher authority (competency), see *supra*—supersedes a lower
level norm when the two are in conflict and the conflict cannot be
avoided through interpretation. A statute that violates a constitu-

---

* Translators' note: Creifelds, *Rechtswörterbuch*, 12th ed. (1994). The
German legal dictionary Creifelds includes the following definition under
the entry, *Massregeln der Besserung und Sicherung:* "Under *The Law Against
Dangerous Repeat Offenders*, enacted Nov. 24, 1993 (RGB1. I 995), general controls were authorized, which, concurrent with the penal sanction,
could be imposed as a reaction to the commission of a crime. Unlike the
retributive nature of the penal sanction, general controls were aimed at
reforming the criminal or protecting the community (the so-called "two
track approach": penal sanction and general controls). *Id.*
    3. *See* BGHZ 34, 34; 78, 218.

tional norm, e.g. runs contrary to a fundamental right, is invalid. The same applies to a legal directive or regulation that contradicts the constitution or formal statute.

Attempts have been made to solve even those norm conflicts that occur within the same statute by referring back to the hierarchical relationship of the norms. This question of ranking only comes to bear, however, when the conflict cannot be resolved according to the principle, *"lex specialis derogate legi generali."*

The notion of ranking norms within the text of the statute itself was developed in the theory of "unconstitutional constitutional norms." It is conceivable that, based on the clear intent of the framers of the constitution (*Verfassunggeber*), certain constitutional norms precede others in rank. Accordingly, Article 79 III of the Constitution (GG) precludes the legislative body charged with making constitutional changes from making certain fundamental constitutional decisions. From this, one can suspect that constitutional framers wanted to give these fundamental norms a higher ranking over other constitutional provisions.[4] Since, however, the constitutional framers themselves, regardless of these weightings, enacted special provisions relating to the basic norms they drew up, conflicts are normally to be addressed by way of the special provisions according to the previously mentioned rules.[5]

Finally, the question has arisen whether a provision of positive law violating a super-positive principle of equity or justice can be invalid. The Federal Constitutional Court has recognized the existence of such super-positive law (binding on the constitutional "givers"), and declared itself responsible for invalidating contravening positive law.[6] However, this conflict rule does not have a reasonable chance of being enforced in every legal order.[7]

When no other conflict rule applies, *conflicts between norms of the same rank*, can be either be declared invalid insofar as they contradict one another, or they simply cannot be applied — the less severe and more appropriate option.

---

4. BVerfGE 1, 32; otherwise BVerfGE 3, 231.
5. BVerfGE 3, 232.
6. BverfGE 3, 232 et seq.
7. Zippelius, 2003, § 6 IV a. E.

f)   Conflict rules also are a product of the chronological order in which the norms come into existence. As a matter of principal, newer law supersedes older, conflicting law (*lex posterior derogate legi priori*). This is so, for example, that a newly enacted post-revolutionary state constitution replaces the previous one—not on the grounds of any formal logic, but primarily due to other considerations, e.g. the prerequisite that a valid constitutional order must also be an effective one (has a chance to be applied and enforced); or the prerequisite that the constitution-giving power (the parliament, the people) can create new valid constitutional law at any time. (*Cf.* §4 III.)

As it relates to simple statutes, as well, the newer norm sets the older, conflicting norm out of service; and this occurs even when the newer norm does not explicitly overrule the older norm. This operates on the assumption that the existing statute can be amended by the legislature; if this is not the case, the older statute is not amended by the newer. This rule of conflict is not applicable as it relates to the relationship between constitutional law and simple statute because the constitution, as higher-level norm, cannot be amended by a simple statute. When a newer statute does not cover the same substantive area to the same extent, it is logically possible that the older norm partially remains valid concurrent with the newer statute. However, it can become clear in such cases that the newer statute shall fully replace the older one, i.e. shall be a comprehensive new regulation of the affected substantive area. Whether this is the case is to be measured according to the intent of the newer statute.

g)   Conflict problems within the positive law are intertwined, to a large degree, with problems of interpretation. Whether norms come into conflict with one other also depends on how they are interpreted. Here, the classical rules of interpretation instruct that norms should be interpreted, to the extent possible, in a way as to avoid contradictions.[8] Striving for statutory interpretation that con-

---

8. Zippelius, 1996, Ch. 38 V.

forms with the constitution, and an interpretation of regulations that conforms with statutes, is related to this aim. Further, the effort to separate equally ranked norms from one another (fundamental rights provisions) so that they may exist without conflicting with one another is related to this aim (§ 10 III).

The question of interpreting statutes in a manner that conforms with the constitution demonstrates the problems involved in such considerations: When the constitutionality of a statute is being reviewed, the issue is not whether one of several possible interpretations of the statute is in harmony with a constitutional norm that has always had clear and defined contours; rather, the issue is whether one of the possible interpretations of the statute is compatible with a permissible interpretation of the constitution. Not only the statute — to which the constitutional standard is applied — but also the standard itself, is not a precisely defined norm, but one capable of — and in need of — interpretation. Consequently, interpretive leeway often allows several arguable interpretive and definitional alternatives (§ 16 II). Then the question arises — leading into constitutional/political problems — whether the legislative or judicially preferred interpretation should be authoritative — that is, who has primacy over defining constitutional norms.

As it relates to the lex-posteriori rule, it is possible that the interpretation emerges that a norm should precede or abrogate another (logically compatible) provision; the latter happens, for example, when the newer norm is to be interpreted as completely regulating a particular substantive area.

Chapter III

Interpreting, Supplementing, and Correcting Statutes

Interpreting a statute means ascertaining the meaning of the words found within a legal text, namely, the facts, values, and prescriptive ideas that those words seek to describe (§ 4 I). This legal information regarding the prerequisite to a legal consequence, as well as the legal consequence itself, cannot always be completely exact. This is not only because the meaning of legal ideas is seldom clearcut and unambiguous, but even if such clarity were possible, language, as the means of communication, brings obscurity into the process.

§ 8. The "Classical" Interpretive Criteria

Literature: F. K. v. Savigny, *Juristische Methodenlehre*, G. Wesenburg, Ed. 1951; F. K. v. Savigny, *System des heutigen Römischen Recht I*, 1840; U. Huber, "Savignys Lehre von der Auslegung der Gesetze in heutiger Sicht," *JZ*, 2003, 1 et seq.

Savigny's "classical" theory of interpretation held that it is the task of interpretation to "place oneself in the legislator's state of mind and attempt to simulate his actions." Interpretation is "the reconstruction of the ideas that reside within the statute."[1] To be sure, Savigny was not concerned with the highly personal ideas of those who participated in the legislative process; rather, he was in-

---

1. Savigny, (1840) 213.

terested in the ideas that the legislator must have had as a "representative of the *Volksgeist*."[2] We wouldn't be far off in our result today if, based on the understandings of democratic legitimacy, we were to formulate the view, according to which the goal of interpretation is to determine what the ideas of the legislator were, and to do this in a manner that is capable of consensus (§ 4 II c). To aid him with his interpretive goals, Savigny developed various interpretive criteria (methods of determining meaning), namely: "grammatical," "logical," "historical," and "systematic," guides.[3]

"Grammatical" interpretation identifies the meaning of the words that make up the text of a statute; it does this according to the common linguistic usage of the community and the rules set forth by the legislature. In other words, one investigates the "feasible meaning" of the words, i.e. the range of meaning the text of the statute has. This range of meaning is limited by linguistic conventions or definitions. "Logical" elements, however, also play a role when it comes to determining the meaning of definitional terms.

These "logical" elements were of particular importance for Savigny. By "logical" elements, he meant the logical relationships that connect together the individual parts of a legal thought.[4] Syntactic connections, in which the individual words of a statute relate to one another, are indeed part of these relationships. But also a part of these relationships are the logical connections through which a norm is combined with legal definitions and supplementary provisions to form the complete set of facts that serve as the basis for the solution of a case (§ 9 I). The (likewise logical) relationship that a legal norm has with the complete context of a legal order's re-

---

2. Savigny, 39, 44.
3. For more on the history leading up to this Canon see: B. Maasch, *Auslegung von Normen, Zeitschrift für das gesamte Handelsrecht* 148, 1986, 360; Raisch, 1995, 72 et seq.; Schröder, 2001, 57 et seq., 141 et seq., 210 et seq.
4. Savigny, 214.

maining norms was characterized, however, by Savigny not as a "logical," but rather, a "systematic" element of interpretation.

"Systematic" interpretation aims to place individual legal ideas within the context of the overall legal order, or as Savigny stated, they are placed "within the internal context that links all legal institutions and rules into a larger entity." Savigny referred to this systematic context because "only when we are clear about what a statute's relationship with the overall legal system is, and how the statute is to work within the system," can we understand the thoughts of the legislator.[5] The argument for this type of interpretation is therefore persuasive because, through systematic interpretation, the will of the legislator is emphasized and stated more precisely.

The notion that legal norms stand in theoretical context with one another, however, yields further interpretive arguments: It is necessary to preserve the "consistency of law"; that is, that individual statutes are so to be interpreted as to avoid logical discrepancies, and to justly balance the differing purposes of conflicting norms. At a minimum, the norm to be interpreted must fit, in conformity with its meaning and purpose, within the context of equal or superior norms. The argument that actually justifies this is found in the requirement of preserving legal certainty and avoiding inconsistency, balancing conflicting goals fairly for all participating interests. Systematic thinking is reasonably scaled back with such a reserved method of interpretation, avoiding impermissible exaggerations.[6] One such exaggeration, for example, could be found in Savigny's method, whereby the entire legal order was to be understood as a conceptual-logical system, as well as the recognition and portrayal of the inner context or relationship "by which the individual legal concepts and legal rules were linked together as a larger entity."[7]

---

5. Savigny, 214.

6. *See* Zippelius, (2003), § 38.

7. Savigny, (1840) XXXVI, 10; For a more candid discussion *see* G. F. Puchta, *Cursus der Institutionen*, vol. 1, 10th ed. (1893) § 15.

Laws not only have a systematic context, but also a historical one. Savigny taught that the law is an apparition of the *Volksgeist*, and this connection with the common conscience also perseveres "as time moves on"; i.e. the law grows with the people.[8] According to this view, the "historical argument" obtains its justification through the will of the people, which develops and manifests itself historically. The law has its "natural source" in the will of the people: the people who created the state and the law as well. And as the people develop, so too does the law.[9] Despite all the reservations one could appropriately have with respect to this older "*Volksgeist* doctrine," we may well be able to agree that today, based on a democratic-based understanding of legitimacy, the law should be capable of consensus for an overwhelming part of society. For this reason, we are justified in asking which interpretation comes closest to the notions of justice that were prevalent when the statute was enacted, while also, however, accounting for changes in these notions (§ 4 III).

Savigny consulted the historical context, as well as the systematic, in order to clarify the creative intent of the legislator; in order to presently recreate and envision the historical context in which the statute was to be interposed; and in order to "illuminate how a statute coexists with the law as a whole," i.e. what a statute's creation and introduction brings to the law as a whole.[10]

§ 9. A Verbal Starting Point, and the Range of a Statute's Interpretation

Literature: *See* § 4 I; A. Keller, *Die Kritik, Korrektur und Interpretation des Gesetzeswortlautes*, 1960; Looschelders/Roth, 1996, 130 et seq.; Ott, 1979, 186

---

8. F. K. von Savigny, *Vom Beruf Unserer Zeit für Gesetzgebung und Rechtswissenschaft*, 1814, 11.
9. Puchta, §§ 9 et seq., 34.
10. Savigny (1840), 214.

et seq. (Berichtigung von Textfehlern); Raisch, 1995, 139 et seq.; Rüthers, 2005, § 22 C.

One would have to agree with classical theory of interpretation that any efforts at interpretation must start with identifying the possible meaning of the words in a statute. Logical and conventional elements play a role in determining the verbal starting point.

I. "Constructing" the Verbal Starting Point

Above all, logical elements, as Savigny meant them, are involved in the construction of the verbal starting point. These logical elements include: the relationship the individual legal words have with one another (the syntactic context) and "construction," (carried out with logical means from a basic set of facts and additional definitional and supplemental provisions, § 6) of the "complete" legal norm to be applied in a particular case.

Legal definitions are included in the provisions that must be applied as a necessary element. For example, when applying § 823 I BGB, an element of § 276 II BGB must also be included: "A person acts negligently if he fails to exercise ordinary care." In applying § 958 I BGB, the elements of § 872 BGB are drawn upon: "A person who possesses a thing as belonging to him is [the owner thereof]." Thus we see that such a definition translates a term into a synonomous combination of several elements that further circumscribe the term. Here, the legislator has "definitional freedom"; he is not bound by extra-legal scientific terminology. To the dismay of Linnés, Art 1 I and II of the Bavarian Fisheries Law of 1908 once legally defined "fish" as: "fish, crabs and other valuable sea creatures, insofar as they are not subject to hunting laws." Extra-legal scientific terminology, however, is significant once it is presumed that a law intended to appropriate and utilize such terminology.

Another way of circumscribing is used where terms such as, "property," "foreign objects," or "unlawful," are raised to the level of factual elements. They represent the result of a legal analysis. When, for example, a legal norm requires the element of "property," the legal criterial must be fulfilled under which title to a thing is obtained. The legal norm thus directly includes all the legal criteria necessary (under another provision) to acquire property. Similarly, the element "unlawful" assumes that no defense exists (§ 6 b).

Section 249 et seq. BGB demonstrates how a *legal consequence* is determined. In this case, the example deals with liability to pay damages for an injury caused to another. First, the complete structure of requisite factual elements and legal consequence provisions, which attach to the "basic facts of the case" in the manner already described, form the complete norm to be applied in the case at hand. This structure forms the "verbal starting point," from which further interpretation proceeds. This describes of course only a simplistic thought process. On closer inspection, one observes that in supplying the norm structure, hermeneutical considerations frequently interpolate. Quite often, only once the element of a norm in need of supplementation is interpreted, do we determine which additional provisions are to be included as supplements.

II. Conventional Linguistic Meaning

Literature: Bydlinksi, 1991, 467 et seq.; Demko, 2002, 117 et seq.; O. Depenhauer, *Der Wortlaut als Grenze*, 1988; Engisch, 2005, 93 et seq., 101 et seq., 123; Hassold, as in § 10 II, 218, 222; Larenz, 1991, 320 et seq.; Raisch, 1995, 139 et seq.; U. Scheffler, "Wortsinngrenze bei der Auslegung," *Jura*, 1996, 505 et seq.; R. Wank, *Die juristische Begriffsbildung*, 1985, 17 et seq.

a)   All further efforts at interpretation start off with a structure of words — held together by syntactic and logical relationships — that is not capable of definition by resorting to legal definitions or other provisions (I). Words not already defined by the legislator obtain their meaning by looking to the common linguistic usage of the community.

Words that generally describe facts related to experiences are quite often ambiguous, i.e. they do not carry the same meaning for everyone, and often an individual does not have an exact sense of the word's meaning. This is due to how the words originally obtained their "meaning." It has been shown that words that describe facts related to experiences are introduced and engrained "exemplarily" (§ 4 I). Thus, a person understands a word along a particular range of meaning with which he has learned to associate the word. For this reason, someone who uses a word will often use it with a somewhat different meaning than the person to whom the word is addressed. Even for the individual, a word is usually not introduced to him that carries with it an exact range of meaning (e.g. how many trees constitute a "forest"; at what second does "night" end?). The text thus typically allows for some latitude—or stated differently—a particular range of meaning with respect to the meaning of words, (hereinafter "range of meaning").

Particularly imprecise are words that designate values, such as "against public policy," or "acting in bad faith." They designate a behavior that, according to the prevalent moral views, is given a particular value in a specific way. It is not even usually possible to determine these views with exactitude because only as it concerns the typical, oft-repeated circumstances of life does the opportunity to make judgments capable of majority consensus arise— and these are only determinable with a limited degree of certainty.[1] Here, the courts are often left with no other choice than to gradually define and circumscribe the meaning of a law's words.

The limits of a word's possible meaning are also the limits of interpretation.[2] If the law wants to go beyond these boundaries, it must do so by means of supplemental or corrective legal development, particularly "gap-filling," rather than through interpretation (§ 11). Inquiring into the limits of a word's range of meaning is aimed at ascertaining which meanings can be ascribed to a word on the basis of common usage in the community (to the extent the law does not contain a conflicting conceptual definition). This "common usage of the community" is typically a tacit general understanding of the range of ideas and notions that a particular word should "mean," (§ 4 I). After everything that has been said about

1. Zippelius, 2003 §§ 5 III; 21 II; *See also* Looschelders/Roth, 1996, 198 et seq.

2. *See also* BVerfGE 71, 115; 87, 224.

words being introduced to people "exemplarily," most words are difficult to circumscribe and define with any exact certainty.

Thus, legal interpretation requires the interpreter to choose the meaning (from within that range of meaning) that is correctly attributable to the norm's text.

b)   From the standpoint of legal certainty and predictability, the fact that legal words may have a range of meaning is considered a drawback; however, under the much-overlooked aspect of "legal flexibility," such latitude can be a distinct advantage: This range of meaning allows these general legal words to adapt to the wide and diverse range of legal problems and circumstances of life that the law seeks to regulate, as well as to the changing prevalent social-ethical views. In this respect, changes in a law's meaning can also occur (§ 4 III). This function becomes particularly clear with general clauses; however, the legal word's range of meaning also gives other legal norms flexible countours. These countours allow compromise between the need for legal certainty on the one hand, and the need for fairness and justice under the circumstances, on the other. Aristoteles had something similar in mind when he opined that the law must be like the leaden rule used in making the Lesbian molding; the rule adapts itself to the shape of the stone and is not rigid.[3]

§ 10. The Argumentative Determination of the "Appropriate" Word Meaning

I. Interpretation as a Legitimacy Problem

Literature: *See* § 3 I; A. Aarnio, "Argumentation Theory—and beyond," *Rechtstheorie*, 1983, 385 et seq.; R. Alexy, *Theorie der juristischen Argumentation*, 2nd ed., 1991, 288 et seq.; R. Gröschner, *Dialogik und Jurisprudenz*, 1982, 128 et

---

3. Aristotle, *Nicomachean Ethics*, V 14.

seq.; W. Hassmer, "Juristische Methodenlehre und richterliche Pragmatik," in *Festschrift für H. Jung*, 2007; Höhn, 1993, 175 et seq.; P. Raisch, *Vom Nutzen der überkommenen Auslegungskanones für die praktische Rechtsanwendung*, 1988; Zippelius, 2003, § 39 (Lit.); Zippelius, 1996, Ch. 33.

All further efforts at interpretation proceed on the basis of a word's possible meaning: These efforts are carried out within a range of meaning that is permissible according to linguistic usage (possibly circumscribed by legal definitions). Within this range of meaning, these efforts must determine the correct meaning to be given to legal words. In choosing a particular meaning, it is necessary to justify the choice—that is, provide reasons for choosing it. Thus, it can be said that interpretation occurs within argumentative structures. Detailed analysis of the "classical" interpretive criteria has shown that the historical and systematic context have argumentative weight because they also elucidate the intent and purpose of legislative action (§ 8). In short, the interpretation of laws, i.e. the determination of the applicable meaning to be given to legal words— one that does not go beyond the range of the word's possible meaning—occurs by considering grounds that speak for attributing to legal words this or that particular meaning (*See also* § 16 II). But often the reasons the interpreter gives for having chosen a particular interpretation do not exclude other possible interpretations; so opined the German Constitutional Court: "Interpretation … has the attributes of a discourse, in which even methodically unobjectionable work yields no absolutely correct statements welcomed without doubt or reservation by all experts. Rather, the reasoning and grounds for a particular interpretation are asserted and contrary reasoning juxtaposed, with the best of these finally prevailing." (BVerfGE 82, 38).

Thus we now focus our inquiry on the *legitimizing reasoning* that guides the selection of a particular meaning. The position that legal application occupies within the system and functioning of the state, as well as the overall functions of the law as a whole, provide important reasoning and justifying arguments that are drawn upon in undertaking interpretive considerations. But in particular, the rationale behind interpretive considerations is obtained from the notion that that the law provides rules of conduct that are free from conflict and provide guidance that is certain, which then fairly and valuably satisfy competing interests. Under a "functional" understanding of law, legal interpretation should be guided by the following arguments (the discussion is demonstrative and by no means exhaustive): Interpretation must take into account that in the state, functions are divided and performed separately. Interpretation should realize the regulatory purpose of the legislator (II) because those charged with applying the law need not only be mindful of the legislature's lawmaking power, but also must consider the legislature's purpose and goals behind its decisions.

Moreover, interpretation must preserve the "consistency of the law," namely, seek solutions that are compatible with the law as a whole—at a minimum, with equal and superior norms (III; *see also* § 7). A norm should be interpreted to fit in a logical and compatible manner within the context of equal and superior norms. In addition, the purpose and ideas of justice embodied in different norms should be in basic harmony with one another. Under the requirement that there be clarity, it is desirable to interpret the same words in the same manner (terminology consistency). (*See* § 10 III a).

Last but not least, the law—and interpretation as well—should regulate justly (§ 10 IV), and optimally satisfy competing interests (§ 10 V).

The considerations discussed above already demonstrate that legal interpretation would be fundamentally misunderstood if we were to understand it simply as, "the reproduction of something already done."[1] We hardly need a contemporary treatise to formulate such a view: "Legal interpretation means not only looking behind that which is expressed in order to obtain meaning, but

---

1. Müller, 2004, No. 249.

also means choosing the correct and authoritative meaning from any number of which are possible."[2]

II. Arguments on the Basis of a Law's Underlying Purpose (Teleological Interpretation)

Literature: *See* § 4 II; Bydlinksi, 1991, 449 et seq.; Demko, 2002, 126 et seq., 133 et seq.; Engisch, 1997, 95 et seq.; Fikentscher, 1976, 674 et seq.; 1977, 364 et seq.; G. Hassold, "Strukturen der Gesetzesauslegung," in *Festschrift für K. Larenz*, 1983, 226 et seq.; U. Köbl, "Allg. Rechtstheorie," in *Festschrift für das Bundessozialgericht*, 1979, 1014 et seq., 1019 et seq.; Kramer, 1998, 110 et seq.; Larenz, 1991, 328 et seq.; Looschelders/Roth, 1996, 153 et seq.; Nawiasky, 1948, 135, 137; Raisch, 1995, 145 et seq.; M. Sachs, "Die Entstehungsgeschichte des Grundgesetzes als Mittel der Verfassungsauslegung," *DVBl.*, 1984, 73 et seq.; Wank, 2001, § 7.

A particular legal and political model for guiding social processes tends to be the basis of legal regulation: When the legislator prescribes certain behaviors, he intends thereby to achieve certain goals. In so doing, the legislator exercises regulatory discretion. On the one hand, it does so with respect to the goals to be reached and their limits; on the other hand, with respect to the expediency (suitability) of the legal methods to be used in order to achieve these goals. Laws are to be interpreted in conformity with the law's purpose. In this respect, pursuant to *subjective interpretation theory*, the ideas of purpose and expediency held by the legislature are authoritative (§ 4 II).

However, *objective interpretative theory* too must hold that it is the legislature's domain in choosing one purpose or another, and to control the manner in which such purpose is realized. Particularly in a state system founded on the principle of separation of powers, legal interpretation undertaken in harmony with the legislature's decisions relating to purpose and expediency also corre-

---

2. Kohler (*See* Literature at § 4), 125; *See also* R. Ogorek, *Richterkönig oder Subsumptionsautomat?* 1986, 80 et seq., 257 et seq., 273 et seq.; *See also infra* § 16 II.

sponds with a system based on the principle of separation of functions. In the parliamentary state, these decisions are left to a majority of the representatives participating in the law-making process. Under objective interpretation, determining the significance of a legislative decision involves thinking of the individual legislator as occupying the role of a representative, one who, on the basis on his authority, acts in accordance with the notions of justice capable of societal consensus (§ 4 II c). Thus, the objective interpreter interprets the goals and means decisions of the legislature as if they were made pursuant to this guiding principle. When the interpreter then sets out to "artificially recreate," the activities of the legislature (§ 8), he is searching for those ideas — and the ideas therein that were capable of consensus — that the legislator must have had, or was likely to have had, as a representative of the community when he enacted the norm. In this respect, those applying the law also support legitimate representation (§ 4 II c).

The history behind a law's introduction and creation provides important information regarding its intended purpose, i.e. the *historical interpretive criteria.* Some authors distinguish between the historical (genetic) component of a law's creation and the legal tradition the law becomes part of.[3] The historical component of a law's creation and the traditional component are not drastically separate components; this is because the tradition, of which the law becomes a part, often influences the ideal that those involved in the legislative act have in mind when enacting a rule. It is in this manner that all, which has historically come before, is figured in during the creative process of a law; in a narrower sense, it is part of the historical creative process of the law. For example, this is why when there is doubt, "classical" fundamental rights guarantees are to be interpreted — insofar as no valid grounds for a different interpretation exist — in accordance with how the type of right has developed and been passed on historically. We thus get a sense of

---

3. *See e.g.* BVerfGE 72, 389.

ideal influenced by tradition: Human sacrifice and temple prosti-
tution, for example, were never included within the concept of "religious freedom," as it is characterized today in western constitutions.
The history of a law's creation can be found particularly in the legislative material, i.e. from statements in support of the law, and in
the records containing legislative deliberations.[4] The ideas of justice, and the legal and political goals capable of majority consensus expressed during the law's consideration, are legitimate factors
to be taken into account as important arguments in choosing a particular interpretation of the law (§ 4 II).

Information regarding a law's intended purpose can also be gleaned
from the law itself, for example, the preamble or other context, i.e.
the location of the norm within the overall system of the law. In
this case, we also enter into the area of systematic interpretation.

These criteria, however, tend to not always exactly define the
intent and purpose of a law. For the most part, we get less than
a clear picture of the goals and expediency decisions made with
respect to a law by looking to the law itself (consulting the deliberations and history surrounding its creation, and then identifying the law's goals and the expediency decisions made by
enacting the law).

Objective interpretative theory does not end with the history
surrounding the creation of a law, or with the law's enactment;
rather, objective interpretative theory assumes that the meaning of
a law can change over time — as do the prevalent general attitudes
of the time. This change in meaning may oftentimes occur within
the range of meaning that was suitable from the outset in arriving
at a clearer understanding of a law's intended purpose. However,
when clearly recognizable legislative expediency and purpose determinations no longer conform to today's prevalent social or ethical views, a law may legitimately be interpreted in conformity with

---

4. *See* BVerfGE 1, 127 et seq.; 2, 272 et seq.; 51, 108; 57, 263; limited
by: BVerfGE 54, 297; 62, 45 with further evidence.

such views (§ 4 III). In this respect, however, in order to preserve the continuity of the law as much as possible, and to avoid unnecessarily engaging in the act of legislating, an interpretation may not deviate more than is necessary from the recognizable intent of the legislature.

The courts may not exceed these boundaries (by further defining a meaning left open by a law, or a legitimate change in that meaning) and trample into the area of purpose and expediency decision-making. Were the courts to do so, they would be assuming a function reserved to the legislature — the institution, under a state system of separation of powers, that is more competent than the courts to make such legal and political decisions. Legislative and parliamentary bodies typically have at their disposal better sources of information, and as such, they make decisions through the necessary debate and consultation with the public, in accordance with the democratic controls necessary for all political decision-making processes.

III. Contextual Arguments

Literature: Bydlinski, 1991, 442 et seq., 453 et seq.; C. W. Canaris, *Systemdenken und Systembegriff in der Jurisprudenz*, 2nd. ed. (1983) 90 et seq.; Demko, 2002, 64 et seq., 121 et seq.; Engisch, 2005, 95, 209 et seq.

As initially stated, there is also an important objective in preserving the consistency of the law, that is, obtaining an interpretive result that is logically and teleologically consistent within the context of equal or superior norms, and when possible, strives for consistency in its use of terminology. Here, interpretive arguments are extracted from the context in which the several norms relate to one another ("systematic interpretation"). In a larger sense, the task is to understand a law's text as part of a context, and to place the text within the overall meaning of the law, and even of the entire legal system. We must contemplate an overall meaning when we seek to determine the meaning of an individual element. Said Celsus: "*Incivile est nisi tota lege perspecta una aliqua particular eius proposita iudicare vel respon-*

dere."⁵ Thus, we look at the interrelation between a law's individual words and the statements connected to them because they shed light on each other's meanings.

Here, a fundamental insight is brought to bear that plays a role in areas beyond the law: generally, there is an interrelation that gives meaning to a single expression by looking to the overall context within which the expression exists. This is not only true of the relationship between the text of a law and the context of the law in which the individual words of a text are used, but also of the relationship of the law with the overall legal order, and with the prevalent views of the culture within which the law exists. The "spirit of the laws," and culture-influencing contemporary ideas and worldviews (*Zeitgeist*), also play a part in determining one's preliminary understanding and interpretation of individual norms.⁶ On the other hand, individual norms and their interpretation affect the legal culture and have a hand in forming and defining its contours.⁷ Such "circularity of understanding" has been described by Friedrich Schleiermacher: "Within a writing, an individual part can only be understood from the whole; thus, a cursory reading to get an idea of the entirety of a writing is necessary before interpreting it." For their part, individual writings have a particular relationship to the language and the history of their time, as do their individual parts to the entirety of the writing. All that is individual in nature must be understood with reference to the entirety; on the other hand, the whole is also to be understood from the individual parts. In all, "complete understanding lies in this apparent circle, in which every particularity is understood from the generality it is a part of, and vice-versa."⁸ In legal interpretation, the linguistic, logical and tele-

---

5. Digests 1, 3, 24.

6. Zippelius, 2004, Ch. 1 II.

7. Zippelius, 2003, § 6 VII.

8. F. Schleiermacher, *Hermeneutik und Kritik*, F. Lücke, Ed., 1838; new edition by M. Frank, 1977, *Hermeneutik*, Introduction §§ 20, 23. Here we find what has since become a catchphrase comment, namely, that it is the job of the interpreter to "understand something spoken just as well, and

ological criteria, in particular, of a correct meaning, are obtained from the legal context.

a)   On this basis, when in doubt, one tends to assume that a law seeks to make consistent use of language; that is, that the same word used in various, different norms should have the same meaning (*terminology consistency*). Of course, this argument is none too important, particularly when it conflicts with the principle that legal norms and the conceptual ideas underlying them are problem-oriented (§ 10 IV).

b)   Moreover, a norm is interpreted, to the extent possible, as to avoid logical inconsistency with superior norms; but in the case of logical inconsistency, the norm would be invalid under conflict of norms rules (§ 7 e). If possible, an interpretation should be selected that enables a norm's application. If certain interpretations yield inconsistencies, and others not, the interpretation that avoids inconsistency should be chosen. In order to avoid inconsistencies with superior norms, norms are to be interpreted "constitutionally conform," and regulations "in conformity with the laws."

Inconsistencies between norms of equal rank (§ 7 e), as well, are to be avoided to the extent possible.

The relationship between § 119 and § 133 BGB provides a well-known example of how one approaches interpretation: § 119 I states: "A person who gives a declaration of intent, and was mistaken with respect to the declaration's content ... can rescind the declaration." This case arises when a person does not attribute to his declaration the meaning that is otherwise given to it by general trade usage or custom, or by conventional linguistic usage. In this case, the declaration is construed according to an objective standard — the content is given such meaning as can be objectively attributed thereto. The declarant can rescind it, but is then liable for damages. In an apparent inconsistency, § 133 BGB states: "In construing a declaration of intent, the real intent of the declarant shall be examined, rather than adhering to the literal meaning of the expression." If, by "real intent," the subjective meaning is al-

---

then even better than its speaker." (§ 18; similarly: I. Kant, *Kritik der reinen Vernunft*, 2nd. ed. (1787) 370).

ways to be understood, this would be in conflict with § 119 BGB. This conflict is avoided, however, by interpreting § 133 as follows: we accept a particular meaning that, from the totality of the circumstances, as well as with a view towards what the recipient of the declaration views as the identifiable intent of the declarant, even if the declarant used the wrong language or expressions (falsa demonstratio non nocet).

c)   Of course, quite often teleological, rather than logical, considerations play the lead role in the relationship between norms. So that legal issues of similar type are treated similarly, the interpretation of a norm should be brought in harmony, to the extent possible, with the policy goals and notions of justice found throughout the wider legal order. The principle of equal treatment demands congruity of legal judgments within the entire legal order.[9] For this reason, legal interpretation also has an ethical context.

How the law has dealt with comparable competing interests in other legal norms is a question that is asked with this legal-ethical context in mind. For the "interest" school of legal thought, asking this question became the most important approach to creation of legal precedent. The legal-ethical context of the norm to be interpreted includes the full range of ethically-relevant legal norms with which the norm can be compared, and to which it can be said the norm is related. The constitution, with its catalog of fundamental rights most particularly, contains important value judgments, which also must be adhered to when interpreting a law.[10] The legal-ethical context of law in a wider sense includes the notions of justice expressed in judicial decisions and state administrative principles (§ 3 II d). Particularly *general legal principles* (e.g. liability for, and compensation of an injury; good-faith reliance; protection of minors and those lacking capacity) are also included in the legal-ethical context. According to Kant, these legal principles have a "regulative" function, namely, "to focus reason towards a particular goal."[11] In the law, they serve as

---

9. The Constitutional Court (BVerfGE 60, 40) promulgated this rule for parliament. Even parliament may not depart from the principles it has used to solve legal questions without good reason. *See also* BVerfGE 59, 49. Moreover, gap-filling must be guided by the principle of "*system congruity*" (§ 11 I b, II d). Legal development too must be internally consistent (§ 13 II).

10. BverfGE 7, 205; *See also* R. Zippelius/Th. Würtenberger, *Deutsches Staatsrecht*, 31st ed. (2005) § 17 II 2.

11. I. Kant, *Kritik der reinen Vernunft*, 2nd. ed. (1787) 672.

"guiding concepts," (*Leitbegriffe*), particularly in legal interpretation. When a legal norm's identifiable purpose is the realization of a general legal principle (e.g. legal certainty) then that which is to be achieved should be realized to the greatest extent possible.

The ends to which various norms serve as means, and the legal principles expressed in them, often conflict. In these cases, the task of interpretation is to construe norms in such a way that an appropriate relationship exists in which these conflicting principles and goals can be realized.[12]

The fundamental rights guarantees of the constitution relate to and conflict with their own goals in a variety of ways. This is of far-reaching importance, particularly because these rights directly or indirectly influence the rules of interpretation in the sphere of private law. Conflicts may arise, for example, between the right of religious self determination of a child and the parent's rights in parenting an individual's free speech rights and the privacy rights of another;[13] the free speech rights of a tenant who wishes to spread propaganda from his balcony and the property rights of the landlord,[14] the artistic freedom of a graffiti artist who artistically blemishes houses, and the property rights of the homeowner[15] or the rights of a verbal abuser and the personal rights of the abused.[16] In these cases, a just and equitable *compromise*—and one that provides for the most benefit—is sought when determining the limits of the parties' respective rights. While paying particular attention to the "prohibition against excess," (principle of the least intrusive interference and "evasion principle") the question to be asked is whether an asserted right (e.g. free speech rights) can also be enjoyed without either impairing a conflicting right in the first place, or impairing that right less severely) (§ 10 V).

As a result of this approach, defining basic rights becomes a continual discussion about justice, in which the various interpretive arguments are used as a basis in defining and limiting these rights. The interpretive latitude associated with fundamental rights guarantees serves to frame the discussion within which the rights and

---

12. *See* Zippelius, *Allgemeine Staatslehre*, 14th ed. (2003) § 33 II 2.

13. BVerfGE 35, 219 et seq.

14. *See* BVerfGE 7, 234 et seq.

15. BVerfGE, *NJW* (1984), 1294.

16. BVerfGE 30, 193 et seq.; 67, 228.

liberties of one are circumscribed in relation to the rights and liberties of another. Within the limits—partly determined by resort to other interpretive criteria—of these fundamental rights, there is the optimization principle. The optimization principle requires that fundamental rights be realized to the fullest extent possible, and in conformity with the constitutional context relevant in the particular situation.[17] Considering the best way to optimize the realization of fundamental rights must also, to the extent possible, be done in a rationally-structured way.[18] In particular, the principle of proportionality serves as a key concept, guiding the definition and limitations of conflicting rights (§ 10 V).[19]

A note: It has been suggested that in the law one must differentiate between "rules" and principles. Rules are norms that are either applied or not applied in a particular case. Principles, on the other hand, would instruct that a particular goal be realized to the extent possible (which corresponds with what has been said above). If principles are in conflict, deciding the weight to be given each determines the extent to which they are applied.[20] However,

17. *See* BVerfGE 6, 72; 51, 110.

18. *See* R. Bartlsperger, in: *Festschrift für W. Hoppe*, 2000, 146; and generally on the methods of rational consensus-building in the law: Zippelius, 1997, Ch. 8, 9, 11 c.

19. According to Heinrich Hubmanns (*AcP*, 155 (1956) 126), when there is an inevitable conflict of competing interests, both sides must "make due with proportional limitations or repositioning until they can exist side by side. Competing interests, it can be said, have a tempering, limiting effect." Where one interest must give way to a more important interest, "there must be as little detriment as possible; the most gentle means must be chosen—the lesser of two evils; but in particular, more interests than necessary must not be harmed." The chances of success are also considered; thus, there must be a justifiable expectation that, "by impairing one good, the other is rescued." *See supra* at 128. Later, Konrad Hesse formulated a similar compromise idea under the name "practical concordance," which found great resonance. (*Grundzüge des Verfassungsrechts der Bundesrepublik Deutschland*, 20th ed. (1995) No. 72.

20. R. Dworkin, *Taking Rights Seriously*, 1978, Chs. 2, 3; *See also* R. Alexy, *Theorie der Grundrechte*, 1985, 71 et seq.; J. Esser, *Grundsatz und Norm*, 1956, 50, 267.

questions remain. When, for example, the free speech rights of one person collide with the personal privacy rights of another, the question arises: Should we view these conflicting fundamental rights as mere "principles," and seek to find a compromise between them, thereby determining the extent of their respective applications? Or are these fundamental rights "rules," since we do have to decide, yay or nay, whether the fundamental right to free speech or the personal right of privacy has been violated? Do the legal rules here overlap with principles; and in what way do they overlap?

Traditional interpretation theory has difficulty answering these questions. The traditional theory is concerned with conceptually defining the limits and application of legal norms ("rules") also in cases where fundamental rights conflict. Through "teleological interpretation," the interpreter must also include and consider the legal norm's purpose in his deliberations. The realization of certain legal principles is often part of a legal norm's purpose (e.g., the right to personal honor and the respect paid to the intrinsic value of the person; or freedom of speech and the democratic principle of unimpeded debate and formation of political ideas) and as such, the proper degree of importance to be attributed to conflicting legal principles is considered when interpreting.

In short: Even when the substantive reach of conflicting legal norms is defined, the interpreter must decide at the same time the degree to which they are defined and limited. This typically is done through teleological interpretation, which is often a principle-oriented interpretation. It is in this manner that legal norms ("rules") and "principles" overlap.

d)   Finally, a legal norm's location in the "overall system," of an individual law may provide particular, though not incredibly important, interpretive arguments—not merely with respect to the inner consistency of the law, but also the intent of the legislature. An example of this is whether § 258 BGB is applicable to a claim for delivery under § 985 BGB. Take the following example: "Collector" loses a valuable stamp. "Finder" finds it and takes it to an appraiser. An employee of the appraiser negligently destroys the stamp. The collector demands that the judgment-proof Finder, who is unable to return the stamp, assign his (Finder's) right to damages from the appraiser to him (Collector). Section 285 BGB provides: "if, as a result of a circumstance under which § 275(1) to (3) relieves the obligor of the obligation to perform, the obligor obtains a … claim for damages for the object owed, the obligee may demand … assignment of the damages claim." This provision is located, however, in the second book (law of obligations), whereas the claim for delivery is located in the third book (property law). This distinction speaks against categorizing the possessor against whom a delivery claim is made as "obligor," and the thing to be delivered as "object owed," within the meaning of § 285 BGB.[21] But these arguments, made from the point of view of the "outer" system, are conducive to comparison and juxtaposition with opposing reasoning from the point of view of the "inner" system — that is, reasons taken from general legal principles found throughout the law as a whole. For example, some might view § 285 as expressing the legal notion of surrogation, which has developed in other legal areas (e.g. in the law of future interests, inheritance law, family property law, capacity of a minor, and execution of judgments). It would be commensurate with this general legal notion to apply the surrogation principle in an expanded interpretation of § 285 BGB to the delivery of property claim as well.

IV. Arguments of Justice

Literature: *See* § 3 I; Larenz, 1991, 348 et seq.

Guiding the selection and weighing of interpretive arguments by asking what is fair and just is commensurate with the law's function in finding just solutions to legal problems (§ 3). This means favoring the arguments that would lead to a fair and just result in the case at hand. As noted above, when interpreting, we envision a particular result, and this steers the mind in reaching that result (§ 3 I d). One could say that when interpreting a law, the view of what a fair result would be influences — from very early on in the process — the type of arguments made; and these arguments stick with the interpreter throughout his efforts.[22] Typically, however, this happens within the boundaries set by the "range of possible meaning"; within the parameters set by the identifiable purpose of

---

21. *See* BGHZ 75, 208.
22. Lege, 1999, 462.

the law; according to the rules of logic; and pursuant to what is consistent with equal and superior norms (§ 10 VI).

The norms and principles of the law *themselves* provide important evidence of what constitute notions of justice[23] that are capable of majority consensus in society—particularly constitutional norms—but also the law as a whole, including judicially created legal principles and doctrines, and recognized administrative principles. These all constitute the "legal-ethical" context (§ 10 III c), which assumes to represent the prevalent societal views of justice. This assumption is based on the notion that, at least as it relates to the long history of legal development, the views of justice that are prevalent and are retained are those that are capable of consensus for the majority of society (§ 3 II d). "Systematic" interpretation (§ 10 III) endeavors to fit the norm to be interpreted within the context of the views of justice that have heretofore been laid down. A "hermeneutic circle" occurs insofar as the criteria for interpreting the law are gleaned from the law itself, which then, in turn, serve to develop and clarify the law.

The question of *legal tradition* (the historical context) into which the law is introduced, yields evidence of the notions of justice capable of societal consensus. "Historical" interpretation is not only capable of providing meaning through evidence of the intent of the legislature (§ 10 II), but also in terms of providing a full consideration of the issue, provides justice. Further evidence is found in the *legislative materials* (§ 10 II). The legislative materials often indicate which notions of justice and fairness played a role in the discussions and debates surrounding a law; they also indicate which of those notions prevailed.

Of increasing importance, *comparative law* provides support for those notions of justice capable of societal consensus. Accordingly, a common European constitutional culture has devel-

---

23. Zippelius, 2003, § 21 II.

oped in areas such as fundamental rights and public law principles. Even legal principles relating to the cultural family to which a person belongs have become part of the "legal ethical context." It was in this manner that Roman legal practice resorted to legal principles that found acceptance within the wider cultural community— the ius gentium.[24]

In searching for a just interpretation, further evidence is provided—to the extent these express the legal and ethical ideas prevalent in the society—by *custom and usage,* and in the growing *institutions* of social life, such as the traditional family order or in trade customs. Because of these normative components of interpersonal relationships, the "humanarum rerum notitia"[25] is thus an important basis in legal awareness. In this manner, the imprint that the family makes in society, for example, can provide support for a particular interpretation of a family law provision. "Standards," as characterized in the Anglo-American system as aids in finding law, are important here as well. They too function as normative models, guiding social behavior—for example: "the prudent businessman standard, standard of fair trade, permissible press reporting, traffic safety, and work loyalty."[26]

Arguments for a just solution to a problem may yield a "*discussion of the consequences.*" Here, the choice between several interpretive alternatives focuses on asking what the real consequences of a particular interpretation will be, and which of these consequences it is just to prefer.

V. Decision Analyses

Literature: M. Deckert, *Folgenorientierung in der Rechtsanwendung,* 1995; H. Eidenmüller, "Rechtswissenschaft als Realwissenschaft," *JZ,* 1999, 53 et seq.; A.

---

24. The Constitutional Court used both the historical and comparative law arguments in BVerfGE 112, 350 et seq.

25. Digests 1, 1, 10, 2.

26. Esser, 1974, 97.

Gern, "Güterabwägung als Auslegungsprinzip des öffentlichen Rechts," *DÖV,* 1986, 462 et seq.; M. Hensche, "Probleme der folgenorientierten Rechstanwendung," in: *Rechtstheorie* 1998, 103 et seq.; Höhn, 1993, 281 et seq.; H. Hubmann, *Wertung und Abwägung im Recht,* 1977; W. Kilian, *Juristische Entscheidung und elektronische Datenverarbeitung,* 1974, 150 et seq., 207 et seq.; Koch/Rüssman, 1982, 227 et seq.; Looschelders/Roth, 1996, 107 et seq.; Raisch, 1995, 185 et seq.; Th. W. Wälde, *Juristische Fogenorientierung,* 1979; Zippelius, 2003, § 20 III 4.

On the whole, legal interpretation appears to us as an argumentative process of selection and decision-making, focusing often on differing and conflicting goals. Compromises are normally sought that are fair and just, provided that the benefit is to be maximized. Considerations of the kind figure into the general formula used in the analyses behind a decision, as well as in gap-filling; above all, however, these considerations are present during the legislature's deliberations. The purpose of these analyses is to bring to the surface the various factors that play a role in purpose-oriented decision-making. This makes it easier to rationally discuss the various conflicting goals and come to a decision that realizes these goals as optimally as possible, and in the most optimal degree possible.[27]

The law should carry into effect an intended purpose, i.e. allow for the retention or acquisition of certain societal goods, and satisfy the associated interests (needs). It is important therefore to get as complete a sense as possible, at the outset, of the societal goods that will be affected positively or negatively by a decision. The "desirability," or "undesirability," of these effects on each of the affected societal goods is determined first separately with respect to each; this should occur in a manner most capable of consensus. The value to be attributed to the affected societal good in comparison to other goods worthy of protection plays a role here. For instance, we could compare the sanctity of one person, and the free speech rights of another; or the life of a pregnant mother and the life of an embryo. The legal order itself provides evidence as to the value to be given in such

---

27. *See* Hubmann, 1977, 16 et seq., 20 et seq., 145 et seq.

considerations: homicide is punished more severely than abortion, and as such, places more value on human life than the life of an embryo. The degree and intensity of an effect upon the good in the instant case is also relevant. This is so, for example, in pollution cases where the degree and amount of pollution plays a role. The increase in value of a societal good, or the diminution thereof, is also contingent upon the abundance of the good: An anti-pollution regulation that would unduly encroach upon property rights in remote parts of Canada could very well be justified in a German city.

Along with the fundamental "desirability" or "undesirability" questions pertaining to a decision's consequences, questions with respect to the probability a particular decision will in fact bring about these consequences also plays a role. This probability is evaluated according to the laws of nature and social sciences, which also exert influence here. Using factors such as "desirability," (or "undesirability") and "*Probability,*" results in an estimated utility or damage assessment with respect to each of the affected societal goods. The decision's complete evaluative process is measured then according to the sum of all advantages and disadvantages, and in particular, according to the quantity of those societal goods positively affected, and those affected negatively.

A particular decision thus carries with it a number of (potential) advantages and disadvantages. One can convert these decisions into thoughts, that is, one can compare all the alternatives of the decision until an optimal and just compromise between the advantages and disadvantages arises.[28] At the very least, the advantages must outweigh the disadvantages ("principle of proportionality"). Because an improper intrusion fails to yield any utility, it can also not be proportionate to the harm caused. If there are several potential alternatives, all of which are more beneficial than disadvantageous, then the alternative that does not excessively cause harm to the interests involved should be chosen ("prohibi-

---

28. *See also infra,* § 17 b.

tion against excess"). If it is at all possible to fulfill the desired purpose without harming any interests, it is preferable to choose this
solution ("evasion principle"). At first blush, this process appears
to be a tool in maximizing freedom and benefit on the one hand,
and minimizing harm on the other. But upon closer observation,
we see that these considerations also involve difficult questions of
fundamental fairness and justice—questions regarding the prior-
ity of these conflicting freedoms and interests, and the extent to which
they deserve protection.[29]

The extent of a norm's applicability (its conceptual coverage and
scope) is determined with all the affected interests in mind, particularly in cases where norms conflict. In short, interpretation is
also result-oriented. Since an interpretation capable of generalization is sought here, there is a focus on results by way of categorizing that goes beyond the circumstances of the individual case.

However, even here the dependence of a legal decision on the particular facts
of a situation is clear. In different situations, even those that can be categorized,
the purposes and interests associated with those purposes play a role in various quantities and groupings. They may not affect one another; they may
strengthen or conflict with one other, or could soon be increasingly affected
or less affected and demand consideration and attention.

VI. The Relationships between Interpretive Arguments

Literature: Alexy (*See* Literature at § 10 I), 303 et seq.; Bydlinski, 1991, 553 et
seq.; Demko, 2002, 161 et seq.; Engisch, 2005, 100 et seq.; A. Gern, "Die
Rangfolge der Auslegungsmethoden von Rechtsnormen," *VerwArch*, 1989, 415
et seq.; Koch/Rüssmann, 1982, 176 et seq. Larenz, 1991, 343 et seq.

All interpretation, in the strict sense, is limited by the "possible
meaning" of the norm to be interpreted. If the interpreter wants
to depart from this approach (e.g. applying a legal rule to a case
for equal protection reasons when the case clearly does not come

---

29. On the rational structuring of optimization considerations *see* also
footnotes 18 and 19.

within the meaning of a norm; or when the interpreter chooses not to apply a norm to a particular case clearly applicable to the norm because of the norm's meaning) this may not occur by means of interpretation, but rather through supplementary or corrective legal development.

It is also axiomatic that no interpretation is permissible, which clearly runs contrary to the identifiable purpose and goal choices made by the legislature; this would involve the interpreter substituting his own political judgment for that of the legislature (§ 10 II). Insofar as the text's feasible meaning and the identifiable intent of the legislature allow,[30] an interpretation should be chosen that avoids placing the interpreted norm in conflict with superior norms; otherwise, the interpreted norm would be invalid under conflict of norms rules. If possible, the interpreter should seek a result that allows the interpreted norm to remain valid. Even conflicts with equally-ranked norms should be avoided (§ 10 III b).

Within such limited range, interpretive arguments often leave open a question—a choice. Interpretive arguments do not constitute an exact instrument, fully solving questions of interpretation. There are a number of reasons to consider that lie within the range of meaning of a law's words when selecting an argument; these may justify selecting a particular variant with respect to a word's meaning. These reasons may complement one other, but they may also conflict.

For example, it is in the best interest of legal certainty, simplicity, and clarity of the law to make use of consistent terminology. Often, however, this interest conflicts with the "functionality restraints" of legal concepts. This restraint requires legal words to be interpreted in a way that is suitable to the particular legal problem the norm is there to address. The word "negligent" offers an example. If the word "negligent" is used in connection with a claim for damages, the word serves the function of making one whole; if "negligent" conduct is punishable, the same word serves another function, namely, a penal one. In

---

30. *See* BVerfGE 18, 111; 54, 299.

light of these two different functions, the word may be interpreted one way in one context, and differently in another (§ 3 I b).

When interpretive arguments conflict, there is no strictly rational hierarchy between them; however, as in the example above, the arguments may be weighed in a transparent manner — inviting others to try and understand the arguments — and according to the weight then ascribed to each, considered accordingly. The most important guiding principle here is allowing the selection of an interpretive argument to be determined by a search for the most just solution to the problem. In other words: Which of the possible "justifiable" interpretations, according to the rules of the art, lead to the most just solution?

The limits, discussed above, may be breached under certain circumstances when necessary to attain a just solution. The interpreter thus may distance himself from the identifiable purpose and expediency decisions of the legislature, provided there exists a legitimate change in textual meaning (§§ 4 III; 10 II). Under certain circumstances, efforts at "finding the law" may also exceed the limits of the "possible word meaning," and as such, depart from the actual task of interpretation and supplement or correct the law (§ 11 I c).

VII. Open Questions

Literature: U. Neumann, "Juristische Methodenlehre und Theorie der juristischen Argumentation," *Rechtstheorie*, 2001, 239 et seq.; Zippelius, 2004, Ch. 8.

Indeed, interpretation occurs in limited rational forms. However, interpretive arguments often allow some decision-making leeway — the possibility of making choices and judgments. The search for bright line rules with respect to judgments left open by a law tend to lead to, more or less, fragmented ideas largely capable of consensus in the community; these ideas are usually the product of specific cases tailored to specific factual circumstances that arise in daily life. There is often no transition between these ideas; indeed, they often conflict with one another. At every turn it becomes clear that the living societal notions of justice are diverse, incomplete, and not without unresolved contradictions. There exist certain tensions and conflicts even within the structure of fundamental rights; these same conflicts are found between legal principles as well (§ 10 III c). Human life is inventive; it leads us continually into new situations in which justice cannot simply be "found," but must be bold, and created through writing (§ 3 II d).

Legal principles and interpretive arguments serve often only as "key concepts," which aid the development and conceptual structuring of fairness and justice considerations. Questions of fairness and justice are given a specific conceptual template, but are not fully worked out to a solution (§ 3 I c). In short, legal interpretation allows itself to be channeled into rationally-ordered paths, but in the end result often in assessments that cannot be explained rationally. Despite these residual irrational factors inherent in decision-making, the possibilities rational arguments contribute should first be exhausted. Rational arguments place the quest for the correct interpretation within the realm of methodological considerations, and contribute to disciplining judicial evaluations. Legal considerations are organized according to the various reasons in support of them; their nature and characteristics are then captured and expressed as rational models of deliberation. In terms of critical discourse, this enables the reasons for or against a particular interpretation to rise to the surface. Likewise, we see which differences in the weighting of the various reasons influence the result. It was thus once obvious to say that the rationality peculiar to legal exegesis was that its illogicalness was limited to small, pinpointable pockets; therefore, interpretation is broken down into individual elements of thought. Criticism, then, is to be directed at each element in particular spots within the argumentative context.[31]

What has been determined here with respect to legal interpretation, is generally applicable with respect to the evaluation of questions of justice. These questions typically are amenable to rationally

---

31. N. Luhmann, *Rechtssoziologie*, 2nd ed. (1983) 286.

structured debate and discussion, though not to an exact method of resolution (§ 3 I c).[32]

§ 11. Supplementing and Correcting Statutes

Literature: F. Bydlinksi, "Über die lex-lata-Grenze der Rechtsfindung," in I. Koller Ed., *Einheit und Folgerichtigkeit im juristischen Denken*, 1998, 27 et seq.; C. W. Canaris, *Die Festellung von Lücken im Gesetz*, 2nd ed. (1983); Engisch, 2005, 177 et seq., 225 et seq.; Fikentscher, 1976, 718 et seq.; Germann, 1967, 111 et seq.; Ch. Hillgruber, "Richterliche Rechtsfortbildung als Verfassungsproblem," *JZ*, 1996, 118 et seq.; Koller, 1997, 221 et seq.; Kramer, 1998, 137 et seq.; V. Krey, "Zur Problematik richterlicher Rechtsfortbildung contra legem," *JZ*, 1978, 361 et seq., 428 et seq.; Larenz, 1991, 370 et seq.; Looschelders/Roth, 1996, 200 et seq.; Maschke, 1993, 159 et seq.; J. Neuner, *Die Rechtsfindung contra legem*, 2nd ed. (2005); Ott, 2006, 74 et seq.; Rüthers, 2005, § 23; Wank, 2001, § 11; E. Zitelmann, *Lücken im Recht*, 1903.

I. Identifying Gaps in the Law

The most convenient and handy tool in revising and supplementing laws is found in gap-filling. There are two types of gaps one might find in a law. The first type of gap is apparent from the phrasing of the law (hereinafter "phrasing gap"). The second type of gap concerns those gaps that are identified after some evaluation and judgment, for which the rather imprecise, abbreviated designation, "judgment deficiency gap," shall be used.

a)   A phrasing gap exists when, from the plain language of a law's text, there is no complete, identifiable rule of conduct. A well-known example of this is found in § 904 BGB: "The owner of a thing is not entitled to prohibit the interference of another with the thing if the interference is necessary for the avoidance of a present danger and the damage threatened is disproportionately great

---

32. Even in the ostensibly different Anglo-American legal culture, it has been concluded: "We can have a rationally structured, but not a rationally determined system of norms." MacCormick, 1978, 271.

compared to the damage caused to the owner by the interference. The owner may demand compensation for the loss he suffers." This provision thus allows access to the property of another when it is necessary to avoid a danger; it then prescribes compensation to the owner. However, the provision does not state who is to provide the compensation: Is it the individual who undertook the emergency action, or the one for whose benefit such action was undertaken?

b)   *Value-Deficient Gaps* are created when a legal norm is capable of being applied without creating conflicts, but due to considerations of justice demands revision. A judge most often identifies these types of gaps where legal norms have been drafted too narrowly or too broadly, i.e., where they do not include cases where the facts indicate a need for regulation and control, or where the norm includes cases, the facts of which were not meant to come under the norm's purview. For instance, under the original law of obligations of the BGB, a legal basis for a claim arising out of an affirmative breach of contract was wanting because the factual requisites necessary to make out such a claim were not addressed in the law; thus, such a claim was introduced by way of analogy (*See infra*). On the other hand, it can seem unjust to apply a rule to certain types of cases that come within the ambit of the rule's text, (i.e. for which the law states the factual requisites necessary, and the facts of the case can be subsumed into those requisites). It was thought to be unreasonable, for example, to apply abortion provisions, which originally did not provide for any exceptions, to physicians who terminated a pregnancy in order to save the life of the mother. (*See* § 12 II). Here, an exception to the general norm was wanting.

Identifying such value-deficient gaps demonstrates again how the law is conjoined with functionality (§ 3 I b). When a law fails to satisfy its purpose in fairly solving legal problems, the law appears in need of supplementation. Indeed, in identifying, and not merely "filling," these gaps, looking to the legal context plays an important, though not exclusive, role. Identifying gaps usually begins by encountering facts that are not covered by a legal rule, but seem to be appropriately covered by a rule enacted for similar cases. (*See infra*

§ 11 II a). Here, the principle of equal treatment emerges as a tool in identifying gaps. In this manner, identifying gaps acts to uncover caprice and inconsistency within the legal order, and paves the way for their elimination. In the area of legal gaps, the principles of systematic fairness, and with it, "consistency of the law," emerge (*See* § 10 III c), according to which the solution to a legal problem fits within the context of equal and superior norms not only on a logical basis, but also in teleologically consistent manner.

Even the question of whether an exception is missing is evaluated according to the equality proposition: the text of a norm can be too broad, thereby including within its purview cases it otherwise should not, based on considerations of equity and fairness. (*See infra* § 11 II b). In such a case, it is legitimate to remove substantially *unequal cases* from the purview of a particular norm, whether through the introduction of a particular exception, or by way of limiting factual elements ("Restriction").

The realization that a particular rule either fails, or no longer satisfies the needs and circumstances inherent in legal relations — that, in particular, the norm is no longer befitting to the social conditions and customs of the people, and thus fails to meet the law's intended purpose — gives one impetus for criticizing an existing law.[1] Should this criticism legitimize supplementing the law, it must always lead to the determination that in addressing these realities a different rule would be more appropriate than the legal rule at hand. However, even in this case, a court may legitimately base its criticism of a law only on grounds of justice.

c)   Discovering the need to supplement a law on the basis of fairness considerations, however, is only the first step. Whether supplementation should be done politically (de lege ferenda) or according to existing law (de lege lata) is dependent on further considerations:

---

1. *See* Larenz, 1991, 414 et seq.; Looschelder/Roth 1996, 238 et seq., 261 et seq.

Striving for material *justice* demands supplementation of the law. However, several reasons may preclude the judge from supplementing the law herself. By supplementing the law, the judge is functioning in a manner reserved for the legislature under a system of separation of powers. The legislature is in a better position than a court to tackle questions of legal supplementation—considerations that are often highly political in nature—and it does so with more democratic legitimacy, particularly with respect to the necessary debate and conversation with the public. Legislative bodies often do this with far broader bases of information before them. If courts were to correct the decisions of the legislature, they might be dragged into everyday political disputes thereby endangering their authority— one premised on neutrality. Above all, judicial supplementation of the law would conflict with the principle of *legal certainty*: "certainty in guidance" suffers when existing law is not strictly observed. At least until there is an ultimate high court decision on the matter, there is the additional danger that, along with uncertainty, there will be unequal treatment of cases as a result of varying lower court decisions. One must consider these pros and cons in order to determine whether a gap is to be assumed de lege lata.

These considerations have not been made the same way at all times. There are periods in the history of the law in which more emphasis was placed on formalism and legal certainty; other periods tended towards attaining justice based on the individual case. These tendencies define the law, down to the individual court decisions. Consequently, in the heightened willingness to remedy the inequities of the law by identifying and closing gaps, we find the distinguishing mark of an epoch: "the law of fairness."[2]

Looking to the idea that a judge is not only bound by the particular law at hand, but also the law in its entirety, the Constitutional Court sought a solution to this problem (Art. 20 III GG): The judge is also bound by general legal principles as expressed in the constitution, elsewhere in the legal order, or in the "established general societal notions of justice."[3] Courts may develop laws on the basis

---

2. *See* Zippelius, 1997, Ch. 6 b.
3. BVerfGE 34, 287 et seq.; 65, 190.

of this "law" (*see infra* § III), whether by legal interpretation or gap-filling and restriction. (*See infra* § 11 II b). Judicial legal development may depart from the text of a law only when the reasons that speak for a particular "law," carry more weight than do the arguments of separation of powers and legal certainty, which demand strict adherence to a "law." Further, such a departure may be made when the text of the law leaves open the possibility that the legislature did not consider the particular problem at hand, and as such, failed to provide for a rule with respect to it. However, if the clearly identifiable meaning of the law precludes this possibility, then the only remaining option is within the exclusive domain of constitutional law courts[4] to declare a norm invalid on constitutional grounds (constitutional norm control).[5]

This approach can lead to the invalidation of a statute because of its highly unjust nature, regardless of its constitutionality.[6] Statutes that fall within the purview of courts that may strike them down on constitutional grounds must be subject to this type of control.

Legal certainty and separation for powers may strictly preclude judicial gap-filling in particular cases. Thus, the principle of "nulla poena sin lege" (Art. 103 II of the Bonn Constitution) prohibits the use of analogy in penal norms. Even the legal and factual elements of tax laws may not be created or tightened by way of analogy; tax law is created only insofar as the legislature specifically creates it: "per dictum of parliament."[7] Moreover, a judge may not make law to the extent that the constitution reserves such law making power.

II. Filling Gaps

Literature: H. F. Brandenburg, *Die Teleologische Reduktion*, 1993; Bydlinski, 1991, 475 et seq.; Engisch, 2005, 187 et seq.; A. Kaufmann, *Analogie und "Natur der Sache,"* 2nd ed. (1982), (1999, 59); A. W. H. Langbein, *Das Prinzip*

---

4. R. Zippelius/Th. Würtenberger, *Deutsches Staatsrecht*, 31st ed. (2005) § 49 III 1.

5. *See* BVerfGE 2, 398; 71, 105.

6. BVerfGE 3, 232; *See also* Zippelius, 1996, Ch. 13 II 2.

7. BVerfGE 13, 328.

der Analogie als juristische Methode, 1992; Larenz, 1991, 381 et seq.;
Looschelders/Roth, 1996, 258 et seq., 204 et seq.; Schröder, 2001, 249 et seq.

a)   An important category of legal gaps is found when a legal
norm fails to apply to those cases, to which justice and fairness would
hold it must. Such was the case when the Civil Code failed to include any provision addressing affirmative breach of contract cases,
such as the following: A farmer buys a cow from a cattle dealer. The
otherwise conscientious and diligent employee of the cattle dealer
negligently delivers to the farmer an animal stricken with mad cow
disease. The cow infects the farmer's entire drove of cattle, which eventually must be slaughtered. The dealer was capable of providing a
healthy new cow within the time allotted under the contract. The
farmer, however, demands compensation for the damages resulting from the contamination of his entire drove. The Code in its
original form, however, only provided relief in cases of a breach of
an obligation (leaving out of consideration §§ 823 and 831) when the
performance owed became impossible or was delayed, the obligor
was responsible therefore, and the obligee was damaged as a result.
In the instant case, damages arose in a different manner.

Analysis of whether a duty of compensation arose despite the
absence of the norm proceeded by *analogy*. The instant case (no
applicable rule in existence at the time) was compared with those
types of cases for which there was a rule. From the perspective of
trying to provide just relief for damages incurred, it was considered whether the instant case should be evaluated similarly to
those cases. From this perspective, were the causes of these damages (impossibility or delay) immaterial that were specifically cited
in the law? Is it therefore sufficient, as a matter of justice, that
the obligor failed in his obligations in any way and thus damages
the other party? This question was answered in the affirmative.
These new factual elements, developed by scholars and court decisions, were adopted by Parliament in a new 2001 version of the
law of obligations (§ 280).

There lies in the analogy a generalization (*see* § 12 I c), which is
based on a judgment; that is, it was decided that the differences be-

tween the circumstances of the one case, for which there was a legally applicable rule, (for which there was a specific, set of factual requisites) and the circumstances of the other case, which were not grave enough to justify a different treatment of the cases. Stated differently: Simply the remaining (general) common characteristics of the factual elements must justify applying this legal consequence. This confirms the notion that conclusion by analogy applies the principle of equal treatment. Equal treatment, and equal judgment and assessment in the law always imports abstraction from existing inequality from a particular legal point of view.[8] (*See also* § 12 I b).

A special case of this is the "argumentum a minore a maius,"or the "*a fortiori conclusion*." This refers mostly to the requirements of a particular legal consequence. When, for instance, conditions are sufficient to warrant an obligation for damages, then more severe conditions, *a fortiori*, must exist to warrant this legal consequence. A familiar example, often falsely attributed to the "argumentum a maiore ad minus," is the following: when a justified interference in the personal property of another gives rise to an obligation to pay damages (§ 904, sentence 2), then too does an objectively unjustified interference, even if this occurs without fault. The legality of the conduct is no prerequisite to the obligation to pay damages.[9]

b)   On the other hand, comparing and categorizing uncovers cases, which for reasons of justice, must be removed from the purview of an (overly broad and generalizing) norm. The former *Reichsgericht* (Imperial Court) provided a classic example of this with respect to abortion.[10] During the time of the Imperial Court, abortion was punishable without exception. However, applying this provision to abortions that were performed to save the life of the mother didn't comport with the court's sense of the law. The court recognized the law's need for supplementation, namely, the "gap" with respect to the applicable defenses. The court, in a consideration of societal goods, thus formulated an missing exception element as a defense. The revision of an overly broad law was formed

---

8. G. Radbruch, *Rechtsphilosophie*, 3rd ed. (1932) §§ 4, 9.
9. Larenz, 1991, 389.
10. RGSt 61, 252 et seq.

as an *exception element*. It is logically equivalent to supplement the legal elements themselves with limiting markers or characteristics ("Restriction"). For example, the older version of § 142 StGB carried potential criminal penalties, if after a traffic accident, it was determined that a party intentionally fled the scene, although he may have contributed to the cause of the accident. The text of the law, however, went beyond the law's purpose by including those individuals who only injured themselves in an accident. Therefore, courts limited the threat of criminal sanction to those who caused injuries to persons beside themselves as the result of an accident from which they fled.[11] In either one of these forms (special exception element or restriction), we recognize that certain deviations from a basic category makes a norm inapplicable for reasons of justice. The exclusion of particular elements from a general principle acquires importance beyond the particular individual case, and it paves the way for differentiating in the general order of norms. The legislature often adopts the revisions made by the courts.

Exception elements may also be capable of generalization. For example, one could look at the abortion example and the exception discovered there and conclude generally that there should be a defense in cases of emergency, which does not only obtain in abortion cases, but rather is applicable in those cases where a choice is made between conflicting social goods. This could be the case in criminal law, civil law, or even public law. The example demonstrates, incidentally, that it is incorrect to promulgate a bright-line rule. Exception elements are not meant to be applied in a infinitely variable manner.

Up to this point, the discussion has centered on the problem of gaps, which arise on the factual elements side, i.e. the factual elements required of a law are drafted too narrowly or too broadly. In the first case, we were concerned with fixing a legal consequence to factual elements, (facts besides those regulated by the law), but

---

11. BGHSt 8, 263 et seq.

which were judged to be the same as those factual elements. This is illustrated by the following diagram:

$$F_1 \diagdown$$
$$F_2 \diagdown\!\!\!\!\longrightarrow LC$$

Gap problems, however, can also arise on the "legal consequence side." Here, we may be confronted with a set of facts that, besides tying them to one legal consequence, we tie to a second legal consequence. This is illustrated by the following diagram:

$$F \diagdown\!\!\!\!\longleftarrow LC_1$$
$$\diagdown LC_2$$

The "argumentum a maiore ad minus" refers more often to the legal consequence. An individual who fulfills certain criteria and has, as a result, certain powers (e.g., the right to terminate without notice, § 626 BGB) may also choose a less severe option under the same circumstances (e.g., terminate with notice).

d)   It has been shown that in every problem of legal interpretation, there exists a legitimacy problem (§ 10 I). The same applies to "open" legal development, whereby courts exceed the possible meaning of a word, or stay well behind the limits. Even here, one should seek out an argument justifying why the solution found is capable of consensus. For open legal development contra legem (§ 13) the "threshold of legitimacy" is particularly high; it must be made clear and understandable why the reasons for judicial supplementation or correction are weightier than the opposing reasons that counsel in favor of separation of powers and legal certainty. If one approaches this issue in accordance with the views of the German Constitutional Court, then legal supplementation that goes beyond the limits of the law's text, must find its justification in profound reasoning from the "law," whether the reasons are based on constitutionally accepted determinations, or other "established general societal notions of justice and fairness," (§ 11 I c).

The "consideration of societal goods" plays an important role in the justification process, namely: the goal of optimizing the safeguarding of societal goods. Courts, long before Parliament dealt with the issue, found support through considering societal goods, when they justified medically-necessary abortions. Thinking about how to optimally satisfy competing interests plays the lead role when a court, through legal supplementation, seeks to provide a solution (a solution that is better than what has been done heretofore) to a problem that satisfies an urgent and legitimate need. (*But see* § 11 I b). In this manner, German private law has developed the transferable expectancy (*Anwartschaft*).[12]

Arguments of logical and teleological coherence (systematic justice) of the law also play a role. Gap-filling serves, at the very least, to remove caprice and inconsistency from the law, particularly when such systematic inconsistency regularly infringes upon the principle of equality (§ 11 I b).[13]

Arguments of consistency and arguments of justice come together in the principle of equality; the "classical" argument of gap-filling—analogy—rests on this principle. Legal notions already set within a law are thought out to their finality with the aid of the generalizing principle of equality.

Incidentally, this makes it clear how problematic the concept of the "gap" is. Because supplementing the law here is aided by the principle of equal treatment (itself a legal principle), the word "gap" refers, at best, to the Civil Code in the previous example, and not to the legal order as a whole.

If the filling of a particular gap is illegitimate or lacking in legitimacy, it may not be allowed, but could nevertheless become operational law (§ 13 I, IV).

---

12. Larenz, 1991, 416.
13. On system congruity *see also* § 10, n. 9.

§ 12. Comparing Cases by Type

Literature: Bydlinksi, 1991, 548 et seq.; W Hassemer, *Tatbestand und Typus*, 1968, 118 et seq.; S Jørgensen, *Typologie und "Realismus" in der neueren Rechtswissenschaft*, 1971; K. Larenz, "Wegweiser zu richterlicher Rechtsschöpfung, in: Festschrift für A. Nikisch," 1958, 292 et seq.; D. Leenen, *Typus und Rechtsfindung*, 1971; Ott, 2006, 159 et seq.; G. Radbruch, "Klassenbegriffe und Ordnungsbegriffe im Rechtsdenken," *Internationale Zeitschrift für Theorie des Rechts*, 1938, 46 et seq.; Vogel, 1998, § 10 II; Zippelius, 1996, Ch. 9 III 2, 37.

I. Comparing Cases by Type as a Means of Interpretation and Gap-Filling

a)   Comparing cases by type is not a tool used only in gap-filling, but also in legal interpretation. In interpretation, case comparison by type takes place within the legal text's range of meaning. Here, we ask whether a particular problematic case, by virtue of the type of case it is, i.e. its general characteristics, fits within the conceptual scope of the law's text. The questionable case, which we will assume fits within the law's range of meaning, is then compared with those cases that undoubtedly fall within the purview of the norm, that is, the norm can be applied to the facts of the case. We then ask whether the questionable case is to be judged in the same way as these cases and is thus included within the particular legal concept. The question involves clarifying the legal norm; it is not a question of subsumption (§ 16 II). By ascribing, or choosing not to ascribe a questionable, problematic case to a particular norm, we can clarify and circumscribe the conceptual reach of the norm. As such, we feel our way from the "conceptual core" of the norm—and the types of cases included therein—out to the limits of the norm's meaning. In unfair practices law, this can lead, for example, to the boundary between fair and unfair competition (§ 3 of the Law Against Unfair Trade Competition).

In unfair practices law, deciding whether there has been fair or unfair competition is often very easy, and is not subject to any dispute. Unfair competition exists, for example, when there are massive bribes to the buyer of a major client. Fair competition exists when a buyer is merely provided with information concerning the offered goods. However, there is an area of problematic cases, in which designating the conduct as fair or unfair is more difficult. Even where cases share many similar characteristics (e.g. gratuities made to a buyer) there are often substantial differences. For example, there is substantial difference between a gratuity consisting of a large sum of money, and a free pocket calendar. Somewhere between the "clear" cases, the boundary between permissible and impermissible conduct must be found—a boundary that cannot be clearly defined, but only determined through a process of evaluation.

In interpretation, as is the case when filling gaps, case comparison by type begins by setting apart the consistent and differing characteristics of the types of cases being compared. Next, there is deliberative comparison, with the goal in mind of treating substantially equal cases equally, and substantially unequal cases unequally. One must not ignore, however, in light of the commonality of hermeneutic deliberation, the boundary that exists between legal interpretation and gap-filling. This boundary runs though the textual meaning of legal provisions; legal interpretation occurs within the range of meaning attributable to the text. When this boundary is crossed, uncovering and filling legal gaps is being done. This boundary is important because, for reasons of legal certainty, it precludes us from going beyond the text, and in many cases makes this impossible by prohibiting the use of analogy (§ 11 I c).

Notably, Anglo-American law compares cases by type. Such categorization in Anglo-American law serves to identify which case characteristics are dispositive in including more than one case under the same legal rule or principle. Such analysis aims at determining whether the case at hand is sufficiently similar to a previously decided case "in the relevant respects." By "distinguishing," the court asks whether the case at bar is the same as the previously decided case with respect to the facts and characteristics that were dispositive in the court's previous decision. Stated differently, common law lawyers ask whether the principles and considerations that justified the first decision can also be applied to the case at bar, or whether the instant case differs in such a way as to justify a different decision.[1]

---

1. *See* MacCormick, 1978, 185, 190, 219 et seq. Iulianus wrote early on that in finding the law, the aim is to tread towards similar cases "*ad similia procedure atque ita ius dicere*," (Digests 1, 3, 12); or as Bracton said, one should "*a similibus procedure ad similia*." (H. H. Jakobs, *De sim-*

b)   The principle idea behind case comparison by type is equal treatment: treating substantially similar cases equally, and substantially different cases differently. Dissecting the agreement and similarity on the one hand, and the different characteristics on the other, includes deliberative comparison. If one recognizes this as a central paradigm of the deliberative process, it goes without saying that the principle of equal treatment is the heart and soul of legal hermeneutics; at the very least it is an incredibly important form in which a problem of justice is made accessible in hermeneutics.

The question of equal assessment is always asked from viewpoint of the respective legal problem the norm (or precedential principle) is there to address (*see* § 12 II). The issue of equal treatment for men and women with respect to child custody is thus approached differently than with respect to military service.

The next issue deals with the *comparative basis* with which a category of problematic cases is correlated. In gap-filling by way of analogy, the legal norms whose analogical applicability are analyzed serve as the comparative basis. In interpretation, the comparative basis constitutes those types of cases that are clearly covered conceptually by a norm. The questionable case type (but one falling within the meaning of the legal text) is compared with the clear cases. However, it is not always easy to find model cases that can serve as a comparative basis. With respect to the necessary value judgments, these often require painstaking advancement and development. Occasionally, the law itself eases these considerations by identifying the type of case that should serve as a guide.

This is how § 138 II BGB introduced the usurious practice as an example of conduct that is against public policy. Of course, that did not spare the courts the job of advancing and differentiating, by case-type, other types of practices that run contrary to public policy e.g. exploitation of an economic position of power; contracts of adhesion; legal constraints with respect to highly

---

ilibus ad similia bei Bracton und Azo, Ius commune, (Special Edition 87, 1996, IX, 36).

personal matters otherwise reserved to one's personal conscience, particularly with respect to religious affiliation; contempt for legal obligations; gross injury to the common welfare.

Furthermore, an important question arises with respect to the *entity* whose evaluation and judgment is considered the standard by which we assess whether characteristic differences between two compared cases are significant or not. A judge, whenever possible, should not decide a case according to his own highly-personal view of the law, but rather he should do so in his capacity as a representative of the community. Thus, he should first seek to determine which interpretation or supplementation corresponds best with societal notions of justice most capable of consensus (§§ 3 II; 4 II c).

c)   Finally, we consider how *legal concepts* and principles should develop. Once a case has been classified, then a decision has been made that the questionable case should not be included within the purview of a particular norm (interpretation), or within the scope of a legal principle (analogy); or it has been determined that the case should be excluded from the norm's application (restriction; exception element), or that the legal principle does not cover the facts of the case.

Thinking in terms of type comparison thus "experiments" with variations of the "basic case" — the type of case that is clearly included within the purview of the norm. This type of thinking examines these case variations and analyzes which differences between the facts and circumstances of these cases should lead to different treatments. By this we more precisely define those elements and characteristics that are dispositive in deciding on the applicability of a legal provision or legal principle. In this way, the *normative type* itself can also be clarified and made more precise. As such, with respect to the realities of life, we further hone in on and specify the scope and applicability of the legal norm (§ 16 II). This process of specification occurs on the level of the general norms.

This specification can thus be weakened by subsequent or additional law. Specific determinations of "unfair" trade practices are found already in Sections

4 et seq. of the Law Against Unfair Trade Practices. In the example discussed above (§ 12 I a), the legal language could read: "A person acts unfairly if, in the course of his commercial activities, he confers a benefit upon an employee or contractor of a business associate." (*Compare* the statutory elements of the bribery provision of § 299 II StGB).

The specific definition last considered here could itself serve as the starting point and comparative basis for further specifications.

For example, the unfair practices norm we just considered could be limited by the following language: "General customary gratuities of minor value are excluded."

The classifying and comparing method gives normative categories a certain "openness" and ability to further develop. This progressive analysis of the conceptually-material elements and characteristics is reminiscent of how Llewellyn picturesquely described the case law method of legal development: like a tree branch whose twigs are understood as growth.[2] We find in the area of legally and ethically-relevant creating of categories a parallel to Husserl's description of the development of empirical concepts. There too there exists, "along with those characteristics already attained yet an indeterminately open horizon of unknown characteristics (conceptual determinations)." "Empirical concepts change by continuously accepting and receiving new characteristics," commensurate with an empirical idea—the idea of an open and continuously revisable concept."[3] This type of thinking is thus always open to new experiences, in contrast to assuming everything is already predetermined, or for other reasons prematurely generalizing individual insights.[4] Comparing types of cases, as well, is concerned with developing "concepts," namely, continuously defining the "objective substantive idea of the concept," (§ 4 I) (that which is the substance of the concept), which indicates the scope of a norm or

---

2. K. N. Llewellyn, *Präjudizienrecht und Rechtsprechung in Amerika*, 1933, 79.
3. E. Husserl, *Erfahrung und Urteil*, 1939, § 83 a.
4. *See* Zippelius, 2003, § 18 II.

principle's application. Conceptual development can either go the way of generalization, or in the direction of differentiation — separation into special categories.

Generalizing is done through analogical thinking. Comparing types leads here to the equal evaluation of differing cases; differing characteristics are regarded as immaterial and thus omitted. This is the basic form of legal thinking. In this manner, not only are the more general legal principles derived from special norms, but originally the concrete experiences behind legal notions were generalized to substantive principles of the law. This is demonstrated in case law legal systems: In those systems, general norms and principles have developed from individual case decisions (as a result of the legal temperament and sensibilities of generations of educated jurists conscious of the dominate ideas of justice) by way of case comparison and sorting by type.[5]

The method of *differentiation* is used when specific cases are found through the process of comparing and categorizing cases, and justice requires that these cases are removed from the purview of an overly broad norm. For these purposes, the special circumstances requiring a decision that deviates from the rule are subsumed into exception elements or limiting factual elements of the rule (§ 11 II b).

A particularly important method of specifying legal concepts in practice occurs by way of *exemplifying casuistry*. This process, as demonstrated in the unfair trade practices example above, identifies those categories of cases that fit particularly within the scope of a legal concept. Legal commentators devote most of their writings to the specifications made to a legal norm's scope of application, particularly those made to general clauses. This can be called *extensional* conceptual formation, i.e., specifying the concept's scope and application; in contrast, the previously-mentioned *intensional*

---

5. Zippelius, 2003, § 18 II.

conceptual formation achieves its goal once it has specified the characteristics and attributes of the concept.[6]

And so generations of jurists feel their way forward in the knowledge and further specification of the law; they compare and assess categories of cases, in which they are led by contemporary notions of justice capable of consensus.

The preceding thoughts describe a particularly important method — which is dominate in daily practice — of continual development of legal concepts. This does not mean, however, that concepts in the law are created in such fashion without exception. New legal solutions may be creatively *invented* to deal with legal problems.[7]

II. Comparing Cases by Type and Its Interplay with Other Arguments

Case comparison by type has been portrayed as a tool in bringing to bear the principle of equality in interpretation and open legal development. Case comparison by type, however, must also be seen in relation to other interpretive arguments; it can only occur within the realm of the logically possible, and as it pertains to interpretation, within the possible meaning of the text (§ 9 II). Within the residual leeway, interpretation often asks whether the questionable case at hand — from the standpoint of the law's purpose (§ 10 II) — is to be equated to those cases, which undoubtedly fall within the purview of the norm.

During a bar fight, someone throws the contents of his beer stein in the face of another, then hits a bystander in the head with the empty stein. In both cases the stein has been used to inflict a battery. Whether the battery is aggravated depends on whether the beer stein is considered a "dangerous in-

---

6. *See* H. Seifert, *Einführung in die Wissenschaftstheorie*, vol. 1, 2nd ed. (1970), 42 et seq.; M. Herberger/H. J. Koch, "Juristische Methodenlehre und Sprachphilosophie," *JuS*, 1978, 811; R. Wank, *Die Juristische Begriffsbildung*, 1985, 35 et seq.

7. Zippelius, 2003, § 11 III 2.

tionable how a court receives and fills a legal gap, for example, as was once the case with affirmative breach of contract (§ 11 a). These uncertainties diminish to the extent that a particular interpretation or supplementation of a law has prevailed and permeated legal adjudication. To the same extent, the likelihood increases of prevailing in a court with such an interpretation or gap-filling argument. If we denote "guaranteed law" as those norms (including the specification of their meaning and conceptual scope) that have a *high likelihood of state enforcement*, then with it there is created an enforceable interpretation or particular gap-filler with respect to this "guaranteed law." This can happen in gradual steps or in one fell swoop, such as when a court makes a ground-breaking decision. An interpretation or gap-filler that has prevailed in judicial adjudication can reach the same level of reliability as a legislative gap-filler or legal interpretation. This is how, for example, damages for an affirmative breach of contract became no less enforceable than legislatively-created legal norms, long before there was ever a corresponding legal rule enacted by Parliament.

Often, the degree to which a norm, interpretation or gap-filler is likely to be enforced goes hand in hand with what are the prevalent societal notions of justice. The convergence of these legal notions (capable of majority consensus) and guaranteed law corresponded with the ideas of the Historical School: a de facto legal custom should become law only if it is recognized, and according to the *opinio juris*, is believed to be the law within the community (*see* § 8).

In the practice of applying the law, it is not uncommon for a particular legal interpretation or gap-filler to be enforced despite the fact it does not enjoy majority consensus. This happens because it is not noticed by those living within the legal system. The development

---

a gradual recognition of the idea of weighing social goods in the law of necessity.

of our complicated and increasingly unmanageable legal system occurs largely outside the public's field of vision, and thus beyond their ability to consent to it. As such, for many areas of the law, the prevalent understanding of the law as held by the people no longer informs us as to how the law has developed; for that, we must rely on the writings of legal commentators.

II. The Binding Character of Previous Decisions

Literature: U Blaurock Ed., *Die Bedeutung von Präjudizien*, 1985; Bydlinksi, 1991, 506 et seq.; Fikentscher, 1976, 706 et seq., 728 et seq.; 1977, 233 et seq., 241 et seq.; Germann, 1967, 227 et seq.; P. Krebs, "Die Begründungslast," *AcP*, 1995, 181 et seq.; Larenz/Canaris, 1995, 252 et seq.; Th. Lundmark, "Umgang mit Präjudizienrecht," *JuS*, 2000, 546 et seq.; H. Mauer, *im Handbuch des Staatsrechts* III, 2nd ed. (1996) § 60, margin number 101 et seq.; Raisch, 1995, 190 et seq.; G. Robbers, "Rückwirkende Rechtsprechungsänderung," *JZ*, 1988, 481 et seq.; E. Schlüchter, *Mittlerfunktion der Präjudizien*, 1986; Zippelius, 2003, § 23 IV.

Even where legal development has lost its basis in the "tacitus consensus omnium," we are not concerned merely with the development of the likelihood *in fact* of enforcing a particular view of the law. Rather, interpretations and gap-fillers, once chosen by courts, attain a certain binding character; this follows from the principles of *equal treatment* and *legal certainty*. These principles admonish the state to remain true to a view of the law that has been decided upon, and as such is all the more settled, provided overriding reasons do not speak in favor of charting a new and different path than the one already embarked on.[4] In the area of interpretation and gap-filling we find parallels with administrative practice, namely, binding itself by its own discretionary decisions (§ 17 b). In short: once an interpretation or gap-filler is chosen, and it is justified

---

4. *See* BFH, Federal Tax Sheet 1964 III, 558; BGHZ 85, 64; BVerfGE 19, 47. The "independence" of the judge does not relieve him of the duty to follow the principle of equality as "law," (Art. 20 III; 91 I GG). *See supra*, § 10, n. 9.

within the latitudes allowed hermeneutically, it may not be over-ruled without good reason.

If, of course, it turns out that an interpretation or gap-filler was unjust from the start, then it also was *a priori* not within the range of alternatives from which a court could legitimately make a selection. If after the fact, it seems unjust because the understanding of what is just has changed over time (§ 4 III), then often there is an important reason for turning away from prior decisions in the area.

These kinds of reasons can make it clear that it is necessary to depart from prior decisions. It is important, however, that *departure* from a prior decision requires justification. One must always consider whether the reasons in favor of departure weigh heavier than the principles of legal certainty and equal treatment, which suggest sticking to the prior decisions.

In asking whether prior decisions should be overruled or de-parted from, the legitimate interest in change often conflicts with the requirement of continuity. The interest in continuity becomes even greater when prior decisions become more established, and the decisions are relied upon as such. This is determined in several circumstances: the level of the court that issued the previous deci-sion, or the decision of a subsequent court does not create the same continuity expectancy as the decision of the higher court. The re-liance and established-law factors also vary depending on whether the previous decision is viewed as a tentative approach or a "de-finitive" settlement of an area of dispute. Above all, reliance and established-law factors become more concrete through repetition in a line of cases, to the point where "settled law" is created. In many cases we find a flowing transition—a gradual increase in the likelihood that a particular interpretation or "open" legal develop-ment will be enforced and acquire legitimate binding authority. These interpretations or developments can reach the level of reli-ability that a legislative interpretation of the law or legal norm en-joys. At this level, we traditionally refer to this as "customary law."

Under this conception of the law—gradually emerging binding authority—the process of "trial and error" remains for legal adjudication more open than the strict doctrine of "stare decisis." In Anglo-American law stare decisis only binds the lower courts to decisions made by higher courts; the higher courts are free to depart from prior decisions under the fiat: "of not departing from like decisions in like cases without very good reasons."[5]

In the event a high court wishes to depart from a line of cases, it does so occasionally by seeking a compromise between the interests of continuity on the one hand, and change on the other. The court may decide the case in conformity with previous decisions, but indicate that a future change in the law is within sight.[6] But because a judge may not make a clearly incorrect decision, such an action is only acceptable if good, albeit not compelling, reasons for a change exist and previous interpretation or gap-filling still finds justification.

III. The Legitimacy of Continued Legal Development

Literature: R. Herzog, *Staat und Recht im Wandel*, 1993, 142 et seq., 199 et seq.; W. Leisner, *Staat*, 1994, 889 et seq. (Richterrecht in Verfassungsschranken); Th. Mayer-Maly, "Über die der Rechtswissenschaft und der richterlichen Rechtsfortbildung gezogenen Grenzen," *JZ*, 1986, 557 et seq.; J. Schröder, "Zur rechtlichen Relevanz der herrschenden Meinung aus historischer Sicht," in J. F. Baur, ed., *Das Eigentum*, 1989, 143 et seq.; R. Zimmerman, *Die Relevanz einer herrschenden Meinung*, 1983.

The legitimacy question is aimed at determining how a judge may justify a decision; within what limits judicial legal development is permissible; and how it is to take place.

Insofar as a law has decided a legal problem and set the criteria for solving it, the judge is fundamentally bound by these criteria (§ 3 Ib).[7] The rule of law principles of legal certainty and separation of powers promote these criteria. Of course, where the legislature has left a contentious legal question open, a judge may not leave the legal dispute undecided; rather, he must find a solution to it. In rare cases he must do so with respect to a wide area of the law not

---

5. MacCormick, 1978, 227.
6. For criticism: Picker, 1984, 153, 158 et seq.
7. *See* BVerfGE 65, 191 et seq.; 81, 31.

occupied by the legislature, such as was the case after 1953 for the norms of the Family Law, which had become incompatible with Article 3, Section 2 of the Constitution.[8] But even within the interpretational latitude allowed by legal criteria, the judge is tasked with making his own contribution to solving the problem at hand.

Even when the authority of a judge in a matter is limited by legislative decision, there are exceptions: where a law fails its function in justly solving a legal problem (in line with societal standards (§§ 3 II; 10 III c)) the judge has the opportunity, albeit limited, to engage in "constructive criticism" of a law by finding "gaps" and filling them. Departing from the law's text, however, is made difficult by the principles of legal certainty and separation of powers. Such departures must be justified by overwhelming reasons of justice, and in some cases, the use of analogy is strictly prohibited (§ 11 I c, II d).

Within the range of meaning that the text of a law leaves open, the applicable word meaning attributed to the text is to be selected, to the extent possible, according to the "rules of the art," namely, in methodical considerations according to the recognized rules of interpretation. These are nothing more than rules of legitimate law-finding (§ 10 I). With this, we must keep in mind the binding authority of general legal principles, which are expressed in the constitution and legal order as a whole (§ 10 IV). This mandate — thinking and considering in compliance with the rules of the art — is not any less important when it comes to gap-filling, where one reaches beyond the text of the law (§ 11 II d).

Even in those cases where the tools of hermeneutics fail to lead to a clear interpretation, the judge is not free to rule arbitrarily or according to his own highly personal view of the law. Rather, a judge must exhaust all avenues in finding an interpretation or gap-

---

8. Art. 117 I GG; discussing: BverfGE 3, 225 et seq.; *See also* BVerfGE 82, 155.

filler that comports the best with *societal notions of justice capable of consensus* (e.g. fits wherever possible in the existing legal framework and is acceptable to a majority of citizens). Consensus is to be sought in two ways: in keeping with professional legal tradition and the legal sense one expects as a result of training and education, but also considering equal treatment and legal certainty, the appearance of legitimacy is created (§ 13 II). As a representative of a democratic society placed under the rule of law, the judge must always consider the society's broad basis of consensus, that is, he must consider whether his decision is compatible with societal notions of justice capable of consensus (§ 3 II).

Not until all these guidelines have failed to clearly lead to a particular decision (leaving open some latitude in arriving at a decision) may a judge legitimately rule according to his own sense of the law. He may also rule according to his own personal views of a law's purpose; or he may even attempt the legal-ethical venture of developing the law. The actual *justifying reason* behind legal development lies in the law's function of providing justice. This function joins together with the principle of democratic representation to form the basic principle that the majoritarian societal views of justice must be brought to bear (§ 3).

The Constitutional Court[9] found a constitutional expression of this idea in Art. 20 III GG. Here, courts are not only bound by a particular statute, but by the law as a whole. The "law as a whole" also includes the unwritten norms of customary law (generally a part of the overall understanding of the law), as well as the "established general societal notions of what the law is." Beyond the positive dictates of state power, there is also "law" existing beyond that.[10] The interpretation of law through the courts may legitimately develop the law on this basis — commensurate with the prevalent societal notions of justice — as these notions

---

9. BVerfGE 34, 287.
10. *See also* Bydlinski, 1991, 222, 289.

are particularly expressed in the overall sense of the constitutional legal order (§§ 3 IId; 11 I c).

IV. On the Effectiveness of Legal Development Contrary to Existing Rules or Norms

Legal application, however, does not always take the path of hermeneutic virtue. Indeed, it can come to pass that courts and organs of the executive branch go beyond the recognizable meaning of a statute. By doing so, they can make a norm obsolete or assert a unilateral interpretation thereof; they are, however, shaping guaranteed law—the whole of those norms and norm limitations that have a sure chance of being applied and enforced. Guaranteed norms are those that have prevailed and been enforced regardless of any subsequent judicial "reprimand" of their illegitimate origin.

Not only the extreme case of revolution—completely sweeping away the constitutional order and replacing it with another—provides an example of an effective movement, in practice, over and beyond any cognition of the law. Mere legal application, the narrow area to which this discussion is limited, provides examples of where real life can take precedence over a norm or the rules of hermeneutics. There are norms that simply become obsolete (they are no longer enforced from a customary law point of view) because in practice they are no longer obeyed. It also comes to pass that the forces of political reality put pressure on the interpretation of a norm to move in a particular direction, and as such, strong interpretative arguments to the contrary are overridden.

A historical example of this could be found in Art. 48 II 1 of the Weimar Constitution. It provided: "The president of the Reich may take all necessary measures, when the public safety and order in the German Reich is substantially disturbed or endangered, in order to restore public safety and order...." The history leading up to this provision of the constitution as well as the traditional meaning of the provision's text and the identifiable intent of the drafters, spoke in favor of a construing the words "public safety and order" in a narrow sense (if not even a strictly police sense). Within a short time, however, constitutional interpretation in practice gave the words another meaning; it not only stretched the meaning of the term "measures," to include legal directives (i.e. the executive branch exclusively occupies the field and exercises independent and plenary authority) but also reinterpreted the meaning of the words "disturbance of public safety and order" to include economic and social emergencies, financial difficulties, disturbances in the functioning of parliamentary governance, and even the impossibility of attaining the necessary majority in parliament. This reinterpretation was certainly no showpiece of hermeneutics according to the rules of the art, but this interpretation of the norm was nevertheless effective constitutional law.

Chapter IV

Application of Legal Norms

To laypersons, the main application of legal thinking is the formal thought of the syllogism, in which the legal norm is the major premise, the facts of the case are the minor premise, and the valid establishment of the normative legal result for the facts of the case is the conclusion. However, the share of formal logical thinking in legal thought should not be overestimated. The judge's difficult tasks include the discovery and the exact limitations on the establishment of the premises (namely the appropriate statements of law on one side and the determination of the facts of the case on the other side.) Here, Schopenhauer's statement applies: The "difficulty and the danger of erring lies in the setting of the premises not in the pain from the conclusion; this follows necessarily and inherently. But to find the premises is the difficulty and there we leave logic behind us."[1] Therefore legal decisions will be found playing a musical ensemble of premise searching, premise restricting, and premise establishment as well as formal logical thinking.

§ 14. Finding the "Relevant" Legal Norm

I. Methods of "Entry"

Literature: C. W. Canaris, *Systemdenken und Systembegriff in der Jurisprudenz*, 2nd ed. (1983); U. Diederichsen, *Die BGB-Klausur*, 9th ed. (1998) 39 et seq.;

---

1. A. Schopenhauer, *Vorlesungen über die gesamte Philosophie*, Part One, Ch. 3 (*Werke*, v. P. Deussen, Ed., vol. 9, 1913, 361).

K. Rehbock, *Topik und Recht*, 1988; Th. Viehweg, *Topik und Jurisprudenz*, 5th ed. (1974).

Until now, these reflections on interpretation have been focused upon the points where we have already found an "appropriate" statement of the law for the facts of the case. To do so, one must however conduct a search for the relevant statement of the law. Logical considerations play only a subordinate role in this search. The totality of legal norms that belong to a legal system do not alone form a logical system and often permit one, as is seen today nearly to excess, to construct proofs out of a few axioms.[2] Locating the norms with which the resolutions of the cases are approached, cannot therefore follow a purely logical schema. The resolution of a case proceeds from the "basic elements of an offense," and the corresponding supplementary norms are in fact consulted according to the rules of logic (§ 6). But in order to find those norms upon which the case solution is based, a technique of "taking-into-consideration" is required.

a)   The search for the relevant norms will be determined by the question that one asks. Law is the regulation of conduct (§ 1). Thus the *substantive-legal* solution of a legal case regularly begins with the questions of "which precise behavioral duty?" and "which legal norm does this duty establish?" In *civil law*, it regularly concerns an individual duty of behavior, as with the payment of compensation or the non-disclosure of a defect in ownership. The solution then begins with a norm, from which such a duty or (from the point of view of the plaintiff) to which its corresponding claim arises (*"claim method"*). But occasionally what remains (*see* § 1 III) in the foreground of legal duties (with a "legal status"), is a question, as for example, whether one can bring a law suit just to determine whether the ownership of a piece of real estate had

---

2. *See* Canaris, 1983; Zippelius, 2003, § 38 II 3. But the norms of a legal order should well stand in a context free of objection and depict a functional order of human cohabitation. (*Supra*, § 7).

been clearly acquired. Similarly, in the areas of *criminal law* the question typically is asked whether behavior that is criminally punishable therefore establishes a duty of criminal prosecution. From time to time, in *public law* as well as *administrative law*, one may also be interested in the coming about of applicable legal norms, and thus in general rules of behavior. For example, it can be verified whether a statute, a regulation or an ordinance was effectively enacted.

To ease finding the relevant norm, great trouble has been taken to put the legal norms together in the clearest arrangement within the statutes. Often, they are arranged by "statutory matters," which means according to questions of fact and areas of life that are regulated by legal norms. In order to find the liability norms, criminal norms or competence norms one is looking for, one needs only to look in the catalogue of norms, which itself deals with the relevant materials. Each norm is thus listed according to the questions to be solved, as for example in the law of obligations, in the property law of the Civil Code (BGB), in the Trade Law Code (HGB), in the Penal Code (StGB), in ordinances and so forth.

In the most common cases, the jurist knows immediately "where to get started." This means one manages to locate the point of entry without anything further, if not to the applicable norm itself, then instead to the relevant catalogue of norms (with regard to the "field of law"). In other cases it may be necessary to pose questions in a series of stages, feeling one's way toward the relevant catalogue of norms, whereby at each step we consider and compare the facts of the case to the legal consequence. In these instances one begins with a higher level of division (between private law and public law, for example), goes from there to lower levels of division (for example, civil code, trade and business law; and then to something like contract law, property law, or family law), and in conclusion going through the facts in the "area of law" (or even multiple "areas of law") adjudged to be relevant, from which every desired legal consequence can be produced.

That is precisely what is correctly understood as "*topical*" *method*.[3] Where the realm of interpretation applies, we are committed to seek out various arguments of interpretation and to insert them into the circle of considerations. Already in the preceding search for the relevant norm, we followed this method. It presupposes stocks of readily-underlying norms, arguments, or knowledge, which therefore already have their place (*topos*). From these stocks one draws forth that which can be applicable to the thing under consideration. That is the technique of the "*per omnes locos tractare*." For it, the ancients needed to picture someone practically knocking door-to-door in order to elicit something. The role allocation at trial is precisely applied to search through these stocks. Thus for example lawyers and prosecutors play their parts, each from his point of view, so that none of the applicable laws and arguments escapes the court.

For frequently recurring questions, one develops certain pragmatic schemes of questions as mnemonic devices in order to find the suitable legal norm. For example, when a claim for compensatory damages or reparation is being considered, one runs through the statutory claim elements in contract; quasi-contract, tort, strict liability and abandonment.

b)   For reasons of the economy of thought, court procedure has cultivated this exercise first to test whether the *requirements of trial* ("secondary norms") are met before one researches the applicability of the substantive law provisions ("primary" norms). One tests quickly beforehand whether the prospective court of enforcement may lend its hand at all to certain substantive law provisions. It would be uneconomical to bang one's head against the wall over the applicability of the substantive law norms, only afterwards to ascertain that in the case under consideration ("in the matter") the applicability can not at all be bindingly decided.

The requirements of trial (requirements of judgment on the merits) support that one in turn passes through a certain sequence. Its purposes allow it rather to vary from the usual sequence of research. Without a long test, it is easy and quick to grasp that one of the requirements of the trial is missing, so an economy of labor would best dismiss the complaint due to the lack of this

---

3. As established in Zippelius, 2003, § 39 II.

trial requirement, without long debate about the other trial requirements to be considered. This proceeding satisfies the requirements of logic, such that the lack of any single trial requirement is equally valid, regardless of what it concerns, and makes the complaint inadmissible.

II. The Function of the Power of Judgment

Literature: Bydlinski, 1991, 419 et seq.; Engisch, 1963, 14 et seq., 85; J. Hruschka, *Die Konstitution des Rechtsfalles*, 1965.

Let us return once again to the basics: The solution of any individual case begins with those norms that one consults, which presumably apply to the case before him, and which therefore should be seriously considered. Or, as seen another way, it depends upon the application of a concrete case (subject to closer examination) to recognize certain norms. This *ability to classify*, the aptitude correctly to associate the appropriate entry point with the appropriate norm is a result of the power of judgment, the development of which occurs, as Kant once said, not only through instruction, but rather through practice.[4] That is, if one so wishes, the philosophical foundation for one to become a good lawyer is not just through learning, but is also through the practice that is attached to that learning, which means through the practice of the power of judgment.

Incidentally, this ability to classify develops its effectiveness in two ways. It allows us not only to choose from the stockpile of legal norms, but also to select those facts that are "relevant to the law" from the abundant concrete circumstances of fact, thus allowing cases to emerge from either side that interest the lawyer.

The lawyer requires therefore a method of practical application for the power of judgment. The changing allocation between norm and factual behavior usually takes place in a "back and forth wandering glance" (Engisch) among many of the *steps of an advanced selection*, which means that in continually eliminating irrelevant norms, application possibilities and facts, one begins

---

4. I. Kant, *Kritik der reinen Vernunft*, 2nd ed., 1787, 171 et seq.

with mostly just an approximate allocation from the larger area of testworthy norms, applicable alternatives and circumstances of fact that are considered. These possible premises of the judicial decision then increasingly narrow themselves. Upon reflection within included norms some will then be recognized as "not relevant here." The narrowly-selected norms that are called upon will be applicable alternatives formulated with a view to the facts of the case, specified and selected in hermeneutic consideration. On the other side, from the abundance of factual circumstances, the "relevant" facts (that means, subsumable under those norms that have been laid out) will be selected. In all of these steps a varying reflexiveness remains. The concrete factual circumstances around which the interpretation of the norm advances (§ 16 II) are also decided this way, while on the other side the interpreted norm controls which factual circumstances emerge as exclusively relevant.

§ 15. The "Question of Fact"

I. The Question of Fact and the Question of Law

Literature: *See* § 16; H. E. Henke, *Die Tatfrage*, 1966, 138 et seq.; H. E. Henke, "Rechtsfrage oder Tatfrage," *ZZP*, 81, 1968, 196 et seq., 321 et seq.; G. Mitsopoulos, "Die Unterscheidung zwischen Tatfrage und Rechtsfrage," *ZZP*, 81, 1968, 251 et seq.; G. Mitsopoulos, "Zur rechtlichen Bestimmung des Tatsachenbegriffs," in: *Studi in onore di Tito Carnacini*, 1984, II 441 et seq.; R. Nierwetberg, "Die Unterscheidung von Tatfrage und Rechtsfrage," *JZ*, 1983, 237 et seq.; W. A. Scheuerle, "Beiträge zum Problem der Trennung von Tat- und Rechtsfrage," *AcP*, 157, 1958/59, 1 et seq.

The application of statutory law used to boil down to one subsuming the "case" before him, and thus certain facts (s), into the interpreted statutory elements (t). Often included, but not already a "basic fact" of the case, are even a version of the elements of the case, which allows it to be applied immediately to the facts of the case. Such facts directly applied to the elements of the case are often the first to be reached before a chain of extensive provisions (§ 6).

So for example, if we can take the case from § 6 once again, the concept of "ownership" in § 823 I BGB next leads to § 958 I BGB: "A person who takes into his proprietary possession an abandoned movable thing acquires ownership of the thing." That leads us then again to other complementary clauses. The word "thing" is defined in § 90 BGB: "Only corporeal objects are things in the legal sense." Section 90a BGB continues: "Animals are not things ... The provisions dealing with things shall be analogously applied to them, insofar as not otherwise provided." Weightier for our case is § 960 I BGB: "Wild animals are ownerless, so long as they are free." Section 872 BGB defines what is to be understood under "proprietary possession": "A person who possesses a thing as belonging to him is proprietary possessor." Here we have arrived with many words at what the facts demonstrate: with the explicit senses, perceptible facts ("corporeal objects," "animals") and an "internal" fact (namely the will of the person, to possess the thing that belongs to him). Questions of interpretation can still be attached, such as the question of what the contents of the idea are that are labeled with the words "as belongs to him."

Most often a jurist does not resolve the elements of the case completely through legal concepts, but the facts show rather a tacit thinking through these concepts and corresponding facts.

A judge, for example, who presides over a common burglary, will not expand upon which facts must be presented in all of their details, such as that another had ownership, or that the thief was a "stranger" (§ 242 StGB). If it were necessary however, he would be able to trace the thread to the end of the legal concepts, according to that which allows the facts to be subsumed. Indeed, we will soon see that some concessions are to be made even from this position.

All questions that concern themselves with the major premise of the legal conclusion are legal questions. Included therein is not only the explanation of the legal elements of the case, but also those things that are completed and made precise through supplementary legal norms. The question of fact is whether those facts presented fall under the completed and precise major premise. This division between "questions of law" and "questions of fact" does not exclude the possibility that the applicable "major premise" will be specified in hindsight after the facts of the case are deliberated and before they will be subsumed under it (§ 16 II).

One cannot always state the legal major premise completely in "pure" factual concepts, that is, in concepts which have no normative content. How does it occur, for example, that a statute assumes that certain normative agenda in fact are submitted? Let us consider two examples. First, the conclusion of a contract assures (at least according to its basic type) that a contractual partner has will to be bound. Second, whoever wants to acquire a thing for himself must want to possess it "as if it belonged to him," which includes the idea that from now on other persons should not be permitted to take the thing, to destroy it, and so forth. The "legal question" (interpretation of the major premise) in such cases reads: What contents does each normative belief need to have in order to attach a legal consequence? A question of fact is that which is submitted as fact. It appears particularly difficult to prepare the division of legal from factual questions with the application of value concepts. We will soon delve more closely into this problem (§ 16 II).

II. The Establishment of Facts

The court applies legal norms as rules to established facts.

a)   *Facts* are not only observations expressed about objects, but also concrete psychic procedures, for example the desire to murder or a decision to kill, which, as concrete actions, are chronologically orderable.

> Also the majority of ideas of value that are capable of consensus have a "factual component," in which value positions taken will become consummated definite components of the majority, which can be ascertainable, for example, through opinion surveys.[1] They can, as questions of fact, be relevant (§ 16 II a. E.). They already play their main role in specifying the major legal premise, thereby taking part in interpretation (§§ 4 IIc; 10 IV).

How are simple facts *established?* The last factor in any empirical establishment of the truth is individual, direct observations. Individual perception provides a more sure insight of experience, if it stands in a context free of contradiction with other results of experience.[2] Through that context, it distinguishes itself from a de-

---

1. Zippelius, 2003, §§ 5 III; 21 II.
2. R. Zippelius, "Der schwankende Boden der Vorstellungen," *JZ*, 2004, 880.

ception of the senses. So as a result, for example, from the total context of various perceptions (from a summary check of selected perceptions), one knows that a rod that is half submerged in water is not bent, in the way it seems to the eye.

b)   Even if the last factor in all empirical truth is the direct establishment of experience data, not every empirical fact capable of proof must be stated *directly*. They can also be *deduced*, and thus are established from direct connection with empirically-founded rules of experience. With a legal context established thus between the fact s1 (for example: streets, roofs and so forth are wet) and the fact s2 (rain), I can then conclude from among the available facts (streets, roofs and so forth are wet) other facts that have been submitted (that it had rained). In such ways, for example, from locating a jug with a person, an historian can conclude who produced it, and from what production technique. *Circumstantial evidence* will be introduced in similar ways in court. Here too it depends mostly upon "historical" determination in the broadest sense; that means it depends upon the determination of events that have occurred in the past.

These considerations lead to the point that almost all evidence brought before a court is strong "circumstantial evidence." One is reminded by these words above all of an example of the following kind: A pistol's bullet has been found in the head of the deceased Mr. Angel. It carries scoring from the barrel of a pistol that Mr. Dubious has in his possession. From that, a judge concludes according to defined rules of experience with a certain probability that Mr. Dubious shot Mr. Angel.

In complicated cases, the criminologist often models several case hypotheses, which means modeling courses of events that hold the already-known facts together according to laws of experience. (It would be for example thinkable, that Mr. Dubious did not himself do the shooting, but rather the pistol was stolen from him and then again foisted upon him.) The goal is then to find additional data, which one or other of these hypotheses either contradicts or proves, until finally only one hypothesis remains available, which produced the single possible model of analysis of the found facts that fits a law of experience. If in this model the immediately relevant facts to the elements of the case (for example, Mr. Dubious's plot to kill) are contained as condition sine qua non, then this is proven through circumstances. In practice one will let the matter rest, if the fact to be proven cannot be thought through according to human judgment, without the outcome being inapplicable. The occupation of Sherlock Holmes therefore, seen as scientific theory, is a science of experience models and the testing of hypotheses. These models have admittedly not, as in physics, a general legal relationship to the object, but rather, as seen in historical science, concrete courses of events and facts. It concerns itself therefore not with "general" but "singular" hypotheses.[3]

Strictly speaking, even evidence offered through witness testimony is, despite the differing trial language, circumstantial evidence[4] for here also the judge concludes a fact s1 (namely, of the witness testimony) in connection with a rule of experience (that a witness with more or less high probability reports what has actually happened) upon another fact s2 (namely of the communicated event itself). Likewise what others feel and believe can only be derived from observable testimony and circumstances.

In some cases of course, the judge himself can observe the directly established facts of the case (that is, subsumable) facts. He can for example ascertain through "inspection" that the plaintiff's land is receiving disturbing "odors" or "noises" in the sense of § 906 I BGB.

III. The Judicial Establishment of Facts in Particular

Literature: O. Jauernig, *Zivilprozeßrecht*, 28th ed. (2003) §§ 25 et seq.; J. J. Musielak/M. Stadler, *Grundfragen des Beweisrechts*, 1984; C. Roxin, *Strafver-*

---

3. V. Kraft, *Erkenntnislehre*, 1960, 246, et seq.
4. *See also* Engisch, 2005, 59.

fahrensrecht, 25th ed. (1998), §§ 15, 24 et seq.; Vogel, 1998, § 2; Th. Würtenberger, *Verwaltungsprozeßrecht*, 1998, margin number 566, 573 et seq.

a)   The norm, from which the asserted legal result is obtained, can only then be applied if each of the noteworthy facts of the case is "realized," which means for each of the noteworthy facts of the case, a subsumable fact is present. This statement needs more precision: The judge must know, *under which conditions* he has *to accept a fact* as "present," especially as to what degree of certainty they must be established for him. Further, with what means does he himself have to produce this certainty about facts, and above all, who must offer and prove these facts? All of these questions need a normative answer. In short, the judge needs *"rules of operation"* that tell him under which conditions he takes facts as given and after that, subsume them under the relevant legal norm. First, one asks if he possesses complete instructions about how he has to affirm presuppositions. The following "operating rules" apply especially to the legal establishment of facts:

First of all, one asks who has the power to discuss the facts and to be concerned with their proof. The first answer that comes to mind says that the court itself has the means to concern itself with the submitted facts. This *principle of investigation* (principle of inquiry, inquisition maxim, briefing maxim) applies above all in a criminal trial and in the administrative and constitutional law proceedings. The civil trial is controlled by the *negotiation maxim*: Here basically the litigation parties have to present the facts to the court and, if they are in conflict, evidence is introduced from which the court is able to be persuaded from the submission of these facts.

For the establishment of facts, we are less interested in the *means* (direct or indirect) with which the material facts are to be produced. As such sources come into consideration according to today's litigation rules, means of knowledge make these facts generally accessible or otherwise evident (for example, that one week ago in the area around the court, frosty weather had prevailed). Moreover, these facts are made known in court (namely, during an earlier official act of the judge's), or through the testimony of the parties or the accused, witness testimony, factual establishment, expert witnesses, inspections, and the content of submitted documents. Confirming doubt whether there is a rule of experience, according to which an established fact s1 can be concluded upon a direct element of the case s2, the judge can allow himself to be directed by expert knowledge.

We are also interested in the *required degree of certainty*. Formulated exactly, we ask to what degree it must be probable, that a material fact of the case under consideration or already presented may be considered by the court as capable of subsumption? The law can connect to a wider or narrower degree of probability. Of course, it is not entirely free however in these points sub specie justice. So it would be grossly unjust to prosecute someone without sufficient proof or even based on suspicion alone. Only in a proceeding that serves to protect individual interests (such as a civil trial), and thus largely leaves the disposition to the parties, can one in certain cases save the assurance of the presentation of legally material facts from the judge; that is to say, when facts alleged about a litigant are by a litigation opponent himself admitted or accepted as uncontroverted (§ 138 III, § 288 of the law of civil procedure). For other cases it can be justified to support a decision on just a substantiation, which means on the *educated possibility*, that the relevant facts are existent. This degree of probability may be sufficient for certain preliminary decisions, which brings the parties thereto no immediate legal disadvantage (for example for the decision about a witness' right of refusal or about the challenge of a judge), or in certain summary procedures, in which the result is reviewable in a regular proceeding. Viewed from such cases we must allow that German procedural law can validly prove, with the highest possible degree of certainty, only such facts as are accepted. But because historical facts (§ 15 IIb) are hardly imaginable with absolute certainty, it calls for an approximation to this degree of certainty, and thus a *limited-certainty probability*.

The judge decides whether the required degree of probability exists, basically in *free consideration of evidence* (§ 286 of the ZPO, § 261 StPO). Basically that means he is not bound by rules of evidence that are prescribed to him under certain requirements for a fact to be considered proven. Whereas under older procedural law, with the confession of the defendant for example, the judge was compelled to the fiction that each of the alleged facts had been committed, today the judge is free to find such a confession to be believable.

b)   These rules of operation — especially the proof and burden of proof rules — belong (according to an admittedly controversial view) to the legal application norms; namely to the norms prescribed by the type and ways of legal implementation ("secondary norms," § 2).

Beside substantive-legal ("primary") behavioral rules, some legal norms also entail procedural law components. These include, for example, civil law norms that co-determine their linguistic connection over the assignment of the burden of proof. Take for example a legislator who wants to establish a claim for damages due to default upon a precondition that the obligor has delayed the indemnification. Here before him stand two formulation possibilities at his disposal — either he calls the "justification requirement" a requirement for the accrual of the claim (formula 1); or he calls the "non-justification requirement" an estoppel for the claim (formula 2), as for example in § 286 IV BGB. For purely substantive law (that means, for the "premier" rules of performance) both formulae are in their logical sense, completely of the same value. One can steer the procedural treatment only with help of these differing formulae. And so the legislator can expressly or impliedly introduce a general "rule of operation" whereby the judge should affirm an element of the case and the associated legal result only if he is certain that this element of the case is realized. Then if doubt remains at trial as to whether the obligor has defaulted, then with formula 1 the doubt is the burden of the obligee because one of the positive requirements of the claim is not established. With formula 2 the doubt is the burden of the obligor because here it is not certain that the claim's hindrance existed. Linguistic frameworks, which for the "premier" rule of behavior are of the same logical value, can therefore procedurally have a different function.

§ 16. Subsumption and Room for Interpretation

Literature: Engisch, 1963, 22, et seq., 86 et seq.; Looschelders/Roth, 1996, 89 et seq.; Ott, 1979, 93 et seq.

I. The Legal Syllogism

Literature: W. Scheuerle, Rechtsanwendung, 1952, 148 et seq.

Section 306 I StGB defines, among other things: "Whoever sets fire (t_3) to woodlands (t_2) of other persons (t_1)..., will be incarcerated for one to ten years." Section 15 StGB requires a "premeditated act" (t_4). Someone sets fire (s_3) to a 10 hectare forest (s_2), which belongs to another (s_1), knowingly and willingly (s_4). Here each abstract element of the statutory elements of the case (t_1, t_2, and so forth) through an attributable fact (s_1, s_2, and so forth) is put into effect. That means each statutory element of the facts of the case determines a fact that can be "subsumed" under it. Thus the statutory order of legal consequence applies to the submitted facts of behavior.

If one says that here the concrete facts of behavior will be subsumed under the abstract statutory elements of the case, then one clothes the legal considerations in the logical schema of a conclusion (of the modus ponens). The major premise states: "If the requirements t_1, t_2, t_3 ... are fulfilled, then the legal result R applies. The minor premise says: "The requirements t_1, t_2, t_3 ... will be fulfilled through the concrete facts of behavior s_1, s_2, s_3.... The conclusion states: "Thus for the concrete facts of behavior s_1, s_2, s_3 ... applies the legal result R."

Doubt is raised whether facts (such as s_1, s_2, and so forth) strictly interpreted, can be subsumed under abstract concepts (t_1, t_2 and so forth).[1] Indeed subsumed means to ascertain a partial identity.

---

1. *See* Engisch, 2005, 63 et seq.

In this sense, one can subsume a special concept under a general concept, like the concept of the mammal (with the conceptual attributes m_1, m_2, m_3, m_4, m_5, m_6, m_7) under the concept of a living being (with the conceptual attributes m_1, m_2, m_3, m_4). The special concept thus contains all attributes of the general concept (and in that way thus consists of an identity of the attribute) and additionally still special attributes (which the *differentia specifica* constitutes). Where then should a (partial) identity between a concept and a concrete fact of behavior lie?

Assume that a traffic ordinance in a closed neighborhood prohibits honking one's car horn. If then a driver honks his horn, the fact of this sound corresponds with an acoustic expression, the prohibition of which is generally signified and called to memory by the words "horn honking" (§ 4 I). It concerns itself therefore with the correspondence of a semantically-mediated identity.

Signs of value can also assume a mediation role between general thought contents and a concrete fact of the case — for example between the concept of such acts being the most disfavored out of a sense of decency, and the fact that such an act exists. There will be more detail about this point later.

II. Substantiation: Interpretation or Subsumption?

Literature: Engisch, 2005, 64 et seq.; Hassemer, regarding § 12; K. Helberg, "Legitimationskriterien der Rechtsprechung," in: N. Achterberg Ed., *Rechtsprechungslehre*, 1986, 277 et seq.; A. Kaufmann, *Analogie und „Nature der Sache"*, 2nd ed. (1982) 37 et seq.; A. Kaufmann, 1999, 73 et seq.; Maschke, 1993, 131 et seq., 201 et seq.; Vogel, 1998, § 9 I.

In a case of arson, assume that only a small, free-standing, natural pine woods with approximately 50 half-grown trees is set on fire. Here doubt can arise about whether these woods can be viewed as a "forest." Does that determine whether it is to be subsumed under the concept of "forest?" Is this the main problem of subsumption, as is popularly believed? The concrete facts of the case remain firm. If the concept of the "forest" is established as an element of major premise, then the question must be raised whether the stand of trees set on fire is to be seen as a "forest" in the sense of the statute, in the identity relationship between the elements of the major premise and in the asserted facts. But if one tries to consider such a formal relationship unburdened by hermeneutic problems and decisions, one can thus see that an extension of this thought is obviously incorrect.

In truth, the question is to be set not as a subsumption problem, but rather as an interpretation problem: whether a stand of trees of the type under consideration (according to its type) belongs to the range of meaning of the concept "forest" or not (§ 12 Ic). With that, one has the question, whether or not this concept is applicable to the submitted case when it is formulated as an interpretation problem. This would be the correct major premise. The decision of such a question can state something like: Even a smaller freestanding, natural, half-grown stand of trees with approximately 50 trees is already a "forest" in the sense of § 306 I No. 5 StGB. Because one such division pertains to the correct "major premise" and not just the concrete facts of the case or their subsumption, it can also extract meaning for future similar cases. It is also sensible, considering that one formulates it as "leading premise" and records it in commentaries.

Therefore, a fact of behavior in its specific form and the question of its subsumption-ability gives the impetus to weigh and *to make precise* the range of meaning of the *norm — with regard to the submitted facts of behavior.* "Substantiating" the norm takes place with reference to the extant reality of life in a "back and forth wandering glance" between the norm and those facts of behavior relevant to the norm (§ 14 II).[2] The area of validity of the norm will be more nearly prescribed at this juncture with a view to the intended correct solution of the concrete cases.[3] For Gadamer the concrete particular proves itself generally as a "determining moment for the

---

2. Examples from Constitutional Law: BVerfGE 2, 401; 3, 422.
3. Lege, 1999, 461 et seq., which also refers to the logic of Ch. S. Peirce.

content of the general."[4] The combining of the norms in the reality of life is entrusted to institutional legal thinking.[5] Therefore, from this view, legal norms are in any case to be understood and specified with reference to those ordered areas of life.

A newer turn of events finds these older thoughts in the lesson that the "program of norms" is to be substantiated appropriately with a look to the associated real "area of norms."[6]

Similar considerations and formulations are also found in Fikentscher.[7] For subsumption, the legal norm, and thus the major premise, must "be prepared in certain ways with regard to (the) facts of the case;" it needs a last possible concretion of the normative face of the constituent parts of the facts of the case." So one must "substantiate the major premise of subsumption . . . , before a subsumption . . . can take place."[8]

Let us consider that which would be the *question of interpretation* in the previously described ways of a typical case comparison (§ 12). In the submitted case, it goes to whether "this sort of" woods is of equal value to each stand of trees, which doubtless lies in the range of meaning of the statutory concept of "forest." The traditional interpretive criteria (§ 12 II) are applied to the decision of such questions of ordering. The decision whether a fact of behavior, according to its type, orders a norm (that means is related in its conceptual range) or not, will determine the applicable range of the norm itself (§ 12 Ic). It was made clear that smaller woods are also of the type "forest" under consideration in the sense of § 306 I no. 5 StGB (major premise), and if the concrete facts of behavior are ascertained (§ 15), then the following subsumption is even more a triviality.

The *valuation concepts* lead to a subtle problem. For example, according to § 138 I BGB, a legal transaction is void if it is "against public policy" (thus

---

4. H. G. Gadamer, *Wahrheit und Methode*, 4th ed. (1975) 519.

5. Discussed further in Zippelius, 2003, § 4 II.

6. Müller, 2004, Margin number 230 et seq., 248 et seq.; compare K. Engisch, *Zeitschr. f. d. ges. Strafrechtswiss.*, 1978, 664 et seq.

7. Fikentscher, 1977, p. 191, 202, 207.

8. However, Fikentscher (1977) regards it not as a problem of interpretation (372. et seq.)

against the feeling of decency of all fair and correct thinking persons.) Is the application of such a concept a question of fact or a question of law? Or are questions of fact and law here unresolvably intertwined, as will be often maintained? These examples will demonstrate that the interpretation problem as well as questions of fact and questions of law can be formulated.

Formulated as a question of fact it would state whether the concrete legal transactions under consideration from the feeling of decency of all fair and correct thinking persons in fact are to be frowned upon. Such an actual evaluation of the concrete facts would hardly exist, so that the "question of fact" itself can be answered only in hypothetical form presuming that all fair and correct thinking persons would value the fact in this way.

The problem may be formulated as a question of interpretation and thus one categorizes it as a question of law: whether a legal transaction of the present type should be related in the realm to meaning of the statutory concepts (§ 15a), and thus whether it would be valued equally (presumably) from the feeling of decency of all fair and correct thinking persons, as the already clarified cases of legal transactions against public policy. This collection of types is offered to the legal application problem because one will be trying to answer questions of value together with a look to future, similar cases.

III. Justifiable Decisions

Literature: H. P. Bull, *Allgemeines Verwaltungsrecht*, 6th ed. (2000) Margin number 376; Engisch, 2005, 150 et seq., 172; H. Maurer, *Allgemeines Verwaltungsrecht*, 15th ed. (2004) § 7 III; F. Ossenbühl, in: H. U. Erichsen, Eds., *Allgemeines Verwaltungsrecht*, 12th ed. (2002) § 10 III; H. J. Papier, "Zur verwaltungsgerichtlinchen Kontrolldichte," *DÖV*, 1986, 621 et seq.; G. Püttner/F. O. Kopp, in: V. Götz et al., Eds.; *Die öffentliche Verwaltung zwischen Gestzgebung und richterlicher Kontrolle*, 1985, 131 et seq.; C. H. Ule, *Verwaltungsprozeßrecht*, 9th ed. (1987) § 2; H. J. Wolff, O. Bachof, R. Stober, *Verwaltungsrecht I*, 11th ed. (1999) § 31 I, III; Th. Würtenberger, *Verwaltungsprozeßrecht*, 1998, Margin number 25.

The application of law does not occur according to an exact method. The uncertainty of statutory application can be found either in the normative or in the factual premises of the legal syllogism; in other words either in a blunting of the interpretation or in doubt concerning the facts of behavior. Beginning with the legal "major premise," and thus in the *normative premises* of the legal conclusions, one can see that uncertainty remains. The choice between more interpretation possibilities and substantiation possibilities, which lie in the play of meaning, or the decision whether a gap in the statute is to be selected and how it should be filled in, does not always permit one meaning to be made from general persuasive reasons (§§ 10 VII; 11). In such cases some interpretations or gap-filling decisions are more justifiable than others. As "justifiable" these should apply if any of the solutions can be comprehensibly grounded upon (if not compelled by) rational arguments rather than proven through general persuasive arguments. Only then does one of the competing solution possibilities earn the preference.

One also sees that *factual premises* can represent different views. Thus the facts upon which an administrative decision may be grounded will often not be established "with a probability limited by certainty" (§ 15 IIIa). More often, administrative decisions must be released with a narrow degree of certainty. Frequently, it must suffice that the evidence submitted is adequate to justify taking on a certain fact, for example that someone "for the intended activity does not possess credibility" (§ 57 of the employment law regulations) or that a pupil has the capacity to follow the lesson of the next higher class. Also concerning such facts as the intellectual ability of a pupil, one likes to be able to have a variety of opinions, which means it is thinkable that the preference to accept some or other facts is not grounded in a way capable of general consensus.

The question of the *reviewability* of *"justifiable" decisions* is of considerable practical meaning. For example, should an administrative court reverse the justifiable decision of an administrative authority, or can a higher court abrogate the justifiable decision of a lower court?

a)   A *court* reviews the decision of an *administrative authority*, so it intervenes in an area outside of its competence. But are law and lawfulness accomplished if the court overturns a justifiable decision of the administrative authorities in order to put its own (also uncertain) decision in its place? The matter to be decided here is whether judicial control should refer to the normative or to the factual premises of the administrative decision.[9]

Were one to remove the normative premises—for example the interpretation of what the word "suitability" means in a legal norm—from the full right of review, one would thus give up concepts that are advanced for making judge-made law precise. To introduce such legal questions in instances of the highest judicial decision lies in the interest of unified legal application, and thus in legal certainty and equal treatment.

It is also conceivable that one removes only questions of fact from unrestricted review. In this case, judicial control is unrestricted for example in the question of what "suitability" means in general, and is only restricted—that means, in respect of administrative leeway—in the question of whether the subject in fact possesses the necessary ownership, according to the court-pronounced statutory concept. Should one thus entrust the last binding decision about questions of fact, for which submissions one can have differing views, to the administrative authorities or to the court? Many support the idea that in such questions the decision of the administrative authorities should tip the balance. It must be responsible in the area of life for which it is concerned, and for the consequence of the decisions that will be made here. The authorities also often possess a closer proximity to the subject area, and that means a familiarity with the single case and experience in the corresponding area of life; hence the "*humanorum rerum notitia.*" This can give greater credibility to the factual assumptions of the authorities. On the other hand, despite its distant proximity to the subject area, a court prefers also for the decision of facts to seem as trustworthy as possible. In today's constitutional reality, the court stands further outside of the influence of political parties and interest groups than do the administrative authorities. And also thanks to the further distance

---

9. *See e.g.* BVerfGE 88, 56, 61.

from the subject area, the court is less in danger of being aggrieved in its decisions by personal likes and dislikes.

Only methodical deliberation can reveal these arguments. Which ones from among them are to be given precedence, is a legal-political question, which positive law must decide. Due to the power of the constitution, room for "courtfree" judgment is conceded only in limited situations. The stronger the encroachment upon a basic right is sought and the more fundamental the concerned basic right is, the denser the statutory predestination of the decision and the judicial control possibility must be (§ 17 d).

b)   If an appeals court reviews the *decision of a subordinate court*, it is not encroaching in an unknown area of competence. Here too, the bases of legal certainty and equal treatment concern an interest in the clarity of problematic legal questions. Clarifying doubt about the interpretation of legal norms and through that, improving the law, is an essential assignment of the appeals court. That speaks in favor of also allowing the subordinate court to use "justifiable" legal opinions to revise.

With a full appeal (*Berufung*) and remonstrance (*Beschwerde*), the comprehensive review of the preliminary decision is in hindsight a factual and legal analysis; with review of law (*Revision*) and legal remonstrance (*Rechtsbeschwerde*) only the legal review is taken to the next higher instance.

§ 17. Discretionary Decisions

Literature: W. Brohm, "Ermessen und Beurteilungsspielraum im Grundrechtsbereich," *JZ*, 1995, 369 et seq.; H. P. Bull, *Allgemeines Verwaltungsrecht*, 6th ed. (2000) Margin number 399 et seq.; M. Bullinger, Ed., *Verwaltungsermessen im modernen Staat*, 1986; M. Herdegen, "Beurtielungsspielraum und Ermessen im strukturellen Vergleich," *JZ*, 1991, 747 et seq.; P. M. Huber, *Allgemeines Verwaltungsrecht*, 2nd ed. (1997) 121 et seq.; H. Maurer, *Allgemeines Verwaltungsrecht*, 15th ed. (2004) § 7; F. Ossenbühl, in: H. U. Erichsen, Ed., *Allgemeines Verwaltungsrecht*, 12th ed. (2002) § 10; E. Pache, *Tatbestandliche Abwägung und Beurteilungsspeilräume*, 2001; Ch. Starck, "Das Verwaltungsermessen und dessen gerichtliche Kontrolle," in: *Festchr. Für H. Sendler*, 1991, 167 et seq.; H. J. Wolff, O. Bachof, R. Stober, *Verwaltungsrecht I*, 11th ed. (1999) § 31 I, IV. J. Ziekow, Ed., *Handlungsspeielräume der Verwaltung*, 1999.

a)   Discretionary legal decisions are among those acts that are conducted by reason of legal *authorizations*. The discretionary acts are relevant then, if they establish, modify or abrogate duties (§ 1 I). So for example, the constitution authorizes the parliament to enact laws. The municipal code authorizes the municipality to enact statutes. The building code authorizes the competent administrative authorities to be exempt from certain building provisions. The road traffic law authorizes the competent police officers to regulate street traffic, which means to require a certain driving behavior of motorists. Such authorizing norms can allow leeway, as when performing or not performing specific acts, or when choosing from among several possible alternative acts. In such ways, where an authority is empowered to settle concrete cases, it can exercise administrative discretion. Where the issuance of general norms is authorized, a legislative, formative leeway is necessarily allowed.[1]

Administrative discretion, limited by the following considerations, is granted to an authority by statute because the elements of a case to be determined in the future cannot be seen beforehand in all of the details that will be material to the decision. The many ways in which persons live their lives do not permit one, through anticipated general norms, to regulate everything completely and correctly. For that reason the legislator authorizes the administrative authorities — for more certain elements of the case, and in consideration of the regulatory purpose and general discretionary limits — to make a concrete decision after con-

---

1. It is a question of terminological choice, whether with the word "discretion" one designates that everything — even the legislative — has decisive leeway, which itself arises from an empowering (as with BVerfGE 9, 10; 27, 67), or whether one reserves it to administrative discretion and in the other cases from a "formative freedom" (alternatively beside "discretion": BVerfGE 27, 67) or — as befits a constitutional state — one speaks of "formative leeway" (as BVerfGE 69, 160).

sideration of circumstances in individual cases. That means in a case before them, the administrative authorities may become active, remain passive or make a choice between different measures or recipients of the administrative action. With the first discretionary alternative some speak of "resolution discretion," and with the second of "selective discretion," although the comparative terms are deceiving because one also "selects" from an array of regulation variations.

b) *Limits of discretion* tend, at least for administrative discretion, to be established already in the authorizing norm itself. Thus, under certain requirements, § 11 of the administrative enforcement statute authorizes a penalty payment to be imposed upon the implementation of a required action, acquiescence or omission. The statute limits the discretionary leeway however, by setting a minimum and maximum penalty range.

Binding discretion arises not only from the formulated discretionary limits of the authorizing norm, but also from the *purpose*. The freedom of choice is therefore also limited by functional fairness, which means that in making the appropriate decision, the statutory purpose must be fulfilled. Consequently a traffic officer is allowed to choose which of two directions of travel he should stop first and which he should permit to proceed, if the intersecting streets are equally heavily traveled. But if coming toward him in one of the travel lanes is only his girlfriend on a bicycle, and the other lane is congested with traffic, then he must first let the congested lane go. Otherwise he would be acting against the purpose of his regulatory authorization, which is to promote the optimal flow and safety of the road traffic.

Furthermore, discretion is limited not only through the authorizing norm itself, but also through the correct context. This follows from the "primacy of the statute," which means that the exercise of discretion may not contravene a legal norm. The constitutional command to treat all persons equally before the law (Art. 3 I GG) is an especially important limit to discretionary leeway. From it, authorities also establish self-regulation to be bound by their preceding acts (compare also § 13 II). If building authorities, for example, have awarded a building exemption to a citizen, they may not deny a neighbor who is otherwise under the same circumstances, even if without the preceding case they could deny the exemption. (However, "same circumstances" are no longer present, for example if such an exemption is so frequently made that eventually it becomes completely acceptable as the measure of the aesthetic, effluent-technical and so forth.)

The discretionary decision is also bound by the *principles of balancing of interests in a rule-of-law state*, if the implementation of the statutory purpose (and the public interests that follow) demands an encroachment on other (public or private) interests. With the selection of the administrative acts, the stipulated and narrowed interests are weighed against one another through judicial means. The principle of *proportionality* must especially be observed.[2] The benefit of an encroachment must be placed in reasonable proportion of the encroachment to the associated interest, which means the benefit must weigh more heavily (§ 10 V). It goes without saying that an unqualified encroachment yields no benefit and is therefore disproportionate. If there are many encroachments from which to choose, and any one alone would suffice, then the *prohibition against excess* is called for. Under this prohibition, one is to choose those measures in which the contrary interests minimally interfere and which do not exceed the required measure of an encroachment interest. Therefore the most gentle encroachment and thus the most gentle medium is to be chosen. Where it is possible, the solution to favor is the one that achieves the sought-after purpose, without other interests being minimized. (Avoidance principle; § 10 V). — An encroachment must also be *reasonable* for the relevant persons. This point addresses the principle that a rule-of-law state principle is person-oriented. Its reason above all is to attend to the identity

---

2. BVerfGE 69, 169.

of the person, his dignity and self-determination, his resilience and
the offer of individual protection of confidences, resulting in a principle that is blended in many ways with the "objective" prohibition
on excess.

Even the general commitment of state actions to justice and democratic legitimacy (§§ 3, 4 IIc) applies not to the interpretation,
but also to the choice of the correct action alternatives that lead to
discretionary decisions. Administrative discretion legitimately creates a balancing of interests from that, which according to the majoritarian *consensus-capable agendas* of the community, and among
these terms and conditions, is maximally profitable (§ 10 V). In
short, the discretionary decision stands not as free choice, but rather
has to make or at least intend (d) a correct selection between multiple action alternatives.

c)   The discretion discussed up until now regards the choice between different decisions—that means alternative actions—to au-
thorize a single legal norm. This discretionary act follows as a legal
consequence, if the elements of the case for the norm are fulfilled
("*legal consequence discretion*").

The leeway in decision-making can however also be located on
the side of the legislated elements of the case, and thus be gener-
ated from the premises of the legal consequences: If a statute uses
inexact legal concepts or terms, then it enables a *range of meaning
in judgments* when applied. In such cases, some have also spoken
of "discretionary facts of the case" and have asked the question of how
this is comported to acts of discretion. One can go a step further:
Because almost all legal concepts and terms are more or less non-
specific, thus allowing room for play in interpretation, one can ask,
in which relationship one can at all correlate *discretionary acts and
interpretation.* That means that on one side is a choice of comport-
ment (acknowledged as a legal consequence) and on the other side
(to be made inside of the range of meaning of the legislative elements of the case) is a selection between different possibilities of interpretation and substantiation. Despite the necessary existing

differences, here and there in important aspects, this choice has to occur according to the same principles. In both cases one cannot make this choice freely, but rather needs a justification. The choice must observe the limits in which the wording of the applicable norm is drafted, must effect the recognizable intention of the legislator, may not allow itself to be in contradiction to other legal norms and must strive for an optimal and fair balance of interests.

d)   As a result, the search for the correct interpretation alternative takes place not infrequently within the range of meaning among decisions, in which the precedence of one solution over the other is revealed not to be according to generally valid criteria, and thus the selection can be made only according to the personal values and convenience of the decision-makers, or overall only as a "balanced" decision (§ 10 VII). The requirement to arrive at a correct selection (here between alternative actions) serves also in discretionary decisions as a thematic leitmotif. This allows the precise coining of generally valid directives, although in small measures, as with questions of interpretation. The stated guidelines for the use of discretion usually do not immediately identify a very definite solution (decision alternative), but rather give consideration to limits of discretion that permit a range of meaning in a precise individual decision of particularity in the case.[3]

e)   It raises the question of the range in which administrative officials, through acts of discretion and ranges of meaning, may be granted *final decision competence* (§ 16 IV). In addition to that, the following is to be taken from the constitution: The constitutional restriction of fundamental rights and regulation of the exercise of fundamental rights are reserved for the legislature.[4] Thus the legislative predetermination of the decisions must be even denser, the

---

3. Engisch, 2005, 152 et seq., 169.
4. R. Zippelius, Th. Würtenberger, *Deutsches Staatsrecht*, 31st ed., (2005) § 19 III 1, 2. To the specification of the immanent boundaries of fundamental rights, *see* § 19 III 3.

more intensely a fundamental right is encroached upon and the more fundamental the affected right is.[5] Further, when the limits on discretionary actions and the latitude in making evaluations must then be that much stronger; the possibilities for judicial control must thus also be denser.

---

5. BVerfGE 83, 142, 145 (range of meaning); 49, 126, 145 (discretion); 84, 53 (control of range of evaluation); to the constitutional requirements of Art. 19 IV GG: BVerfGE 84, 49.

Chapter V

Logical Formalization and Data Processing in the Law

It is not the task of this introduction to reproduce the extensive special research in the application of logical calculus and data processing in jurisprudence. It would also be impossible to accomplish that in just a few pages. What can however happen in the space available is this: One can sharpen the critical consciousness of the uninitiated for the application of logical calculus, so as to recognize that the efficiency of those methods in jurisprudence always has limits.

§ 18. Logical Formalization in the Law

Literature: C. E. Alchourrón/E. Bulygin, *Normative Systeme*, German edition 1994; G. Kalinowski, *Einführung in die Normenlogik*, German edition 1973; U. Klug, *Juristische Logik*, 4th ed. (1982); P. Lorenzen, "Methodisches Denken," 1968; U. Neumann, in: Kaufmann/Hassemer/Neumann, 2004, Ch. 7; E. Ratschow, *Rechtswissenschaft und formale Logik*, 1998; I. Tammelo/H. Schreiner, *Grundzüge und Grundverfahren der Rechtslogik*, I 1974, II 1977; Weinberger, 1989; G. H. von Wright, *Normen, Werte und Handlungen*, 1994, 19 et seq., 56 et seq.; H. Yoshino, "Über die Notwendigkeit einer besonderen Normenlogik usw.," in *Gedächtnisschrift für J. Rödig*, 1978, 140 et seq.

I. The Notion of a Calculated Law

The law could be obtained to the degree of exactitude it allows itself to be brought to a completely formalized and unambiguous language. For this, one must depict in a formalized way how one assembles complex statements from simple statements. These statements would thus be treated as elements of a calculus, which means of a system that consists of the symbols and the rules for the combinations of these symbols. These rules frame the logical-statement *syntax* of the formalized language. They indicate the relationship in which the symbols will be correlated to one another and how certain symbol combinations in other situations can be transferred. Assume, for example, that in a calculus, these symbols were used: p, q, r, … ; &, →. Then in fact: "p," "q," "r" are used as statement variables, "&" as conjunctor (that means as the logical particle "and") and "→" as subjunctor (that means as "if, then"). It then holds, for example: $[(p → q) \& (q → r)] → (p → r)$.

In a formal calculus the content of the connected symbols has no meaning. Only if one attaches such *meaning* to the statements' variables, does a statement's contents express meaning from the formula. For example, Cleopatra could have considered: [(This object is a bead → this object is made of lime) & (this object is made of lime → this object is dissolvable with vinegar)] → (this object is a bead → this object is dissolvable with vinegar.) The connection of a meaning with any symbol is a question of *semantics*.

A language which expresses something from its contents is thus only exact if, first, the symbols' associated meanings are exactly certain and if, second, the statements are connected with one another according to exact rules. Since the law contains statements of content, that would thus twice presuppose an exact legal language: an exact semantic, with whose help one would be able exactly to define the meaning each word of the statute has, and a formal ability to calculate the correct statement (in respect of its logical structure). Neither presupposition is fulfilled in the law.

II. The Limits of Feasibility

a)   Beginning with the first point of exact semantics, something is already missing. Legal norms demonstrate far-reaching experience in their content. Words, which generally indicate the facts of experience, are however introduced and practiced by example and therefore have an *inexact extent to their meaning*, a "range of meaning" (§ 4 I). Incidentally, even if it were possible, it is very doubtful whether one should strive for a completely exact legal language. That has to do namely with the range of meaning and also the elasticity of legal norms, which, if made exact, would lose their adaptability to the many shapes and forms of concrete conditions (§ 9 II b). Should one however take this adaptability through an exact formulation, during which one must induce — even given the degree of unavoidable semantics — through general clauses that make up the latitude of indefiniteness in the law, in order to carry out the need of a situationally-related account of justice?

b)   Also called into question is whether legal statements lend themselves to the form of a calculus. Usually, calculated statement-logic confines itself to the linking of *factually-described* (*"descriptive"*) *statements*. For example: [(p → q) & p] → q. That means: If a sentence (if p, then q) is true, and if p is true, then q is also true. By comparison, the scheme of a legal norm would read: If p is realized and q is realized, then r ought to (should) happen. Thus, what next occurs is the task of introducing *ought* to the formalized language. At the same time, whether one can connect this shorthand like a descriptive statement to the assumptions of the legislated elements of a case, and thus according to logical rules, raises doubt as to whether the descriptive statements are valid for this connection.[1] These rules, which are further introduced to enable one to go from descriptive statements to descriptive statements, can be either true or false. By comparison, the legal norm connects prescriptive statements to the realization of legislated assumptions, which should be something definite (and not, something which is true.)

The forms of methodical thinking are not limited to descriptive statements. In general, in preliminaries and also outside of traditional logic, one is permitted to introduce rules for a schematic operation, especially rules, according to which one must or may go from

---

1. *See* R. Walter, *Hans Kelsens Rechtslehre*, 1999, 31.

certain sentences to others.[2] Fundamentally, one can thus introduce operative connections for very different types (not only descriptive) of statement forms. Thus one may also schematically depict each formal connection that consists of a command and its factual conditions. One can symbolize the sentence, for example: "If the elements of an offense T are realized, then the action should happen," with E → !a. That does not mean that the command is derivable from E in a logical way, but rather only that if E takes place, the command (!a) also applies.

An important field yet remains however for the rules of assertive logic. They are applicable in any case to the legislated *elements of an offense E*, which can be more exactly stated as the conversion of the expression in which the condition described (E), and under which the command of conduct (!a) applies. This expression (E) may be replaced through another expression to which E is equivalent. T (including any single character of the elements of the case within E) may be further replaced through an expression, which is implied through E-designated terms. In this case, other possibilities of the fulfillment of the elements of the case must however also be left open.

These deliberations permit one to construe lawful "aggregate elements of the case," of which one has need for the solution of a case (§ 6a). It is precisely here that a schematization of legitimate rules can be of service, and it illuminates the relationship of one element to another.

Apply for example the rules:

$(e_1 \, \& \, e_2) \rightarrow \, !a$ and $(e'_1 \, \& \, e'_2) \rightarrow e_2$
then also apply:
$(e_1 \, \& \, e'_1 \, \& \, e'_2) \rightarrow \, !a$
Therefore:
$\{[(e_1 \, \& \, e_2) \rightarrow \, !a] \, \& \, [(e'_1 \, \& \, e'_2) \rightarrow e_2]\} \rightarrow [(e_1 \, \& \, e'_1 \, \& \, e'_2) \rightarrow \, !a].$

---

2. Lorenzen, 1968, 84 et seq.

One can thus depict smaller parts of areas of the law in a formalized way, as here with the context between "basic elements of the case" and subsidiary prescriptions.

c)   The process concerns itself only with the schematization of trivial considerations, in which the main problems of jurisprudence are not located. The observation of the logical rules is certainly a necessary consideration for correct legal thinking. But this does not get us very far. One is reminded of the verse from Wilhelm Busch: "Two times two makes four, that's right. But sadly this is void and passive. I'd rather have it clear, not trite — something that is full and massive." Legal-methodical deliberations must always *grasp beyond pure logical structures*, and precisely there lie the difficult questions. Yet in each semantic question one must leave the field of pure logic, as for example with the simple question, what is to be regarded as a "dangerous instrument" in the sense of § 224 StGB (§ 12 II). It applies even more to cases with problems of things that are absent. In the whole content of its richness and difficulties, the legal order allows nothing to be portrayed as a system of axioms out of which concrete questions of law would be solvable through purely formal operative thought connections (§ 14 I).

It may suffice to make clear once more the example of filling in the gaps: The ascertainment and correction of a *lack of values* in the law is no formally logical affair. The earlier, unconditional criminal offense against hit-and-run driving would be formally without defense even in cases in which the driver injured only himself. That in this case a conditional necessary element of the case is missing, was no pure logical finding (§ 11 II b). Even the first question raised, whether a damages claim would be allowed in the case of the positive breach of contract, is not decided through pure logic. With formal arguments the reverse conclusion would be just as good — which means just as bad — to have been established as a conclusion by analogy. But first the question of equal valuation will lead us further here (§ 11 IIa).

A calculation does not make the value decision dispensable. It can be seen, for example, in the attempt by Ulrich Klug to calculate a *conclusion by anal-*

ogy with the help of classical logic:[3] $[(v'_{1,2\ldots m} \subset v_{1,2}{}^{sim}{}_{\ldots m}) \,\&\, (v_{1,2}{}^{sim}{}_{\ldots m} \subset r_{1,2\ldots n})] \subset (v'_{1,2\ldots m} \subset r_{1,2\ldots n})$. In order to arrive at this formula, one assumes the following: $v_{1,2\ldots m}$ denotes the class of things in the elements of the case, which the prerequisite of a legal norm fulfills (example: the cases of negligent delayed performance); out of this legal norm should arise the legal consequences $r_{1,2\ldots n}$ (example: a claim for damages due to non-performance, right of withdrawal and so forth). The symbols $v_{1,2}{}^{sim}{}_{\ldots m}$ denote then the class of elements, which are similar (sim) to the characteristics of the first class and together with them build a "circle of similarity." The question asks whether the named legal consequence is also applicable to the class of elements $v'_{1,2\ldots m}$ (e.g. the cases of the positive breach of contract.) The answer is as follows: If one accepts that the legal consequences $r_{1,2\ldots n}$ apply to all the cases that belong to the circle of similarity (2nd parentheses), and if the class $v'_{1,2\ldots m}$ belongs to this class of similarity (1st parentheses), then the legal conclusion $r_{1,2\ldots n}$ is valid also for the class $v'_{1,2\ldots m}$ (3rd parentheses).

This works under the conception that there are classes of case facts that are sufficiently similar to the statutorily-regulated class of case facts, and so are therefore within the purview of the legal problem to be answered. For the entire circle of these similar classes of case facts (the "similarity circle"), the statutory legal conclusion should then apply. The clinching question still remains in the decision of values: Which types of case from the statutorily-regulated type of case is similar enough, such that the legal conclusion applies to it?

Again, it boils down to the old question of whether the difference between the regular and the problematic types of cases (within the purview of the solution to legal problems) are insubstantial, so that it is fair to assign the same legal consequence to both types of cases (§ 11 IIa). Thus the "calculating" jurist misses the forest while examining the trees.

§ 19. Electronic Data Processing in the Law

Literature: M. Bartsch, *Datenberarbeitng and Law*, 1990; F. Haft, *Einführung in die Rechtsinformatik*, 1977; F. Haft, "Computergestützte Entscheidungsfindung," in: W. Hoppe et al., Eds., *Rechtsprechungslehre*, 1992, 589 et seq.; A Kaufmann, Ed., *EDV und Recht*, 1973; W. Kilian, *Juristische Entscheidung und*

---

3. Klug, 1982, 135.

elektronische Datenverarbeitung, 1974; Klug, *supra* § 18, 174 et seq.; L. Reisinger, *Rechtsinformatik*, 1977; J. Schneider, in: Kaufmann, Hassemer, Neumann, 2004, 376 et seq.

In the beginning, it had been discussed whether and to what extent judicial functions could be entered into data processing equipment. Initially an exaggerated hope emerged for a calculated law that consisted of exact linguistic and logical elements that would be digestible by data processing devices. This old illusion that the judge could decide like a machine, now takes a technological twist to the machine that will decide like a judge. And so now the debate from conceptual jurisprudence must satisfactorily prove that it was principally incorrect to expect that a judge will work like a machine, that a judge will only "articulate the words of the statutes" and that a judge will apply them according to purely logical operations.[1] For the same reasons and to the same degree that this was incorrect, it is also impossible to let all judicial decisions be carried out through a data processing device. We thus envisage which operations devices could be allowed to take over.

a)   Electronic data processing serves a wide range of functions to store decision fundamentals (statutory texts, judicial opinions and scholarly texts). Here it is concerned with the storage and recall of information. This will be fragmented into bits, exhausting the internal information capacity when it is called upon to decide between two "values." In Morse code it would be the choice between the symbol "." and the symbol "-". With electronic data processing it is the choice between two different electronic voltage states. Through many combinations of these basic units a very large amount of information is reproduced. Not only exact information, but rather inexact information is formed into pure wording (that is the succession of letters), translated into a binary system and then stored. One can even "Morse" a love poem.

---

1. Zippelius, 2003, § 38 II.

With the mentioned grasp of legal decision fundamentals one must also consider the *grasp of pure wording*. One such use of data processing guarantees that appropriate norms and preliminary decisions will not be overlooked and not forgotten and that they are readily available. One can also incrementally scan the data, so that step by step decision fundamentals will always be supplied for the operators' own considerations. This use of electronic data processing approximates the form of a dialogue. Any storage of data has indisputable advantages, not only for judicial application, but also perhaps even more for legislation, where it can avoid contradictions and repetitions.

In adjudication, a quick grasp can particularly serve any number of preliminary decisions and the methods of categorizing the case comparisons as well as cultivate the type differences (§ 12). The necessary collection, screening and differentiation of legally-relevant complex characteristics (case typing) can be facilitated and refined. In this way, just to name one example, one can do something like hold up a large number of matters for comparison against § 3 of the statute prohibiting unfair competition. A new case to be decided will then often match one of the previously-decided case types of unfair behavior.

Comparative matters can also be at the disposal of *legal consequences* (*supra*, § 12 III). So one can, for example, sort sentences concerning certain criminal deeds according to certain criteria, note those for which the sentence is a considerable one, compare the reduced sentences, and in this way strive for an equally-weighted criminal sentence. In similar ways one can guide the award of pain and suffering damages through secure channels: through an increasingly consolidated net of case types (for example bodily injuries and those awarded pain and suffering damages). Here, as well, electronic data processing can safeguard one of large uniformity and security in the disposition of legal consequences—but not more. Of course it is also true that through data processing one cannot "absolutely" (that is, independent from preliminary decisions in comparable cases) ascertain how much pain and suffering damages would be adequate for example, for a six year-old school girl who had been kicked in the left eye. Electronic data processing can thus merely refine that which up until now had been decided with technically simpler means through pain and suffering damages tables.

b)   Yet a case comparison, such as making an approximate assessment of damages for pain and suffering, can only be prepared using electronic data processing—through the retrieval of comparable cases. The subsequent questions of equal valuation can not be solved fundamentally through a calculator. It depends upon whether the remaining differences in characteristics are considerable or whether and in which regards they must lead to a different treatment of the cases compared. Such *evaluations* are not replaceable through stored data and formal connections. Thus, a decision is more likely to be made through electronic data processing if it can be constructed from exact components according to exact rules of operation. But even in such cases, only individual partial operations can be separated out in exact steps (§ 18 II) from the totality of the legal considerations. That permits some calculable operations to be carried out through data processing, such as the pure assessment of taxes, civil service salaries or retirement.

c)   Even user-defined storage and user-defined access to normative and prejudicial decision foundations have a downside. The "*benefit of oblivion*" is lost in this way. The idea of becoming oblivious to preliminary decisions and (increasingly "obsolete") norms, seen in a large ensemble, provides the opportunity for the function of legal revision. It allows certain decision bases to disappear from the field of view. This "daily legal revision," which juridical practice implements through simple nonobservance, is not based on a conscious mental struggle. So it can occur that from case to case, that one becomes oblivious to the bases of fundamentally important decisions, while on the other hand, marginalities remain alive. But by and large, what is controlling in this selection process during adjudication, is what one might call a secondary tendency that makes obsolete those things that are unimportant and untimely for practice.

But above all, electronic data processing neither generates each effort of legal dogma that is routinely found in the commentary and textbook literature, nor does it help to derive that which is important and sustainable from the abundance of the norms and decisions through the modification of the law. Without these accomplishments a jurist runs into the danger of "failing to see the forest for the trees," fails to recognize the position from which he makes his decisions in the complete context of the law, does not comprehend the multiplicity of the interests worthy of consideration (§ 10 IV) and loses himself in marginalities.

Index

The numbers refer to the section numbers and paragraphs thereunder.

a fortiori conclusion 11 II a, c
ability of the law to conform (flexibility) 18 II a
acceptance, *see also* capable of consensus 3 II c
allowing 1 III
analogy 11 II a, 12 I c, 18 II c
analogy (prohibition of the use of analogy) 11 I c
anticipation in interpretation 3 I b, d, 10 IV
application of legal norms 14 et seq
argumentation, hermeneutic 10 II, 12 I
argumentum a maiore ad minus 11 II a, c
argumentum a minore ad minus 11 II a, c
authorizations 1 I, II, 17 a
automatic data processing 19
avoidance principle 10 V
axiological consequence of the legal order, *see also* legal-ethical context 11 I b
back and forth wandering glance, *see* interactions
balancing of goods, *see* balancing of interests
balancing of interests10 V, 11 II d, 17
"basic elements of the offense" and

supplementary provisions 6, 14 I
belief contents, "objective" 4 I
"benefit of oblivion" 19 c
borderline cases
— of interpretation 10 VII, 12 I, 13 I, 16 II, III
— of discretion 17 d
— legal-ethical 3 II d, 10 VII
briefing maxim 15 III b
burden of justification, *see* legitimacy calculus 18 I
case comparison, *see* comparing cases by type
case law 3 I a, 12 I a
casuistic 12 I c
causality, legal 5 I
chance of law enforcement 2, 7f, 13 I, IV
change in statutory meaning 4 III
changes in the meaning of a law 4 III, 10 II
circumstantial evidence 15 II
classificatory thinking 12 I, 16 II
commands, *see* "ought" norms
commitment of administration 17 b
common usage 3 II d, 10 IV
comparative evaluation, comparative ordering 11, 12, 16 II
comparison by type 11 II, 12, 16 II, 19 c

concept formation in tension 12 I c
concepts, conceptual development 1
 I, 9 II, 12 I c
conditional program 5 I
consensus capacity of legal decisions
 3 II, 4 II, 10 IV
consequence-oriented interpretation
 10 IV, V
constitutional
—- conforming interpretation 7 g,
 10 III b
—- violation of constitutional
 norms 7 e
constructions in the law 6, 9 I
context, interpretation out of — ,
 see also legal ethics 10 III
continuity of jurisdiction 13 II
corresponding application, see analogy
customary law 3 I a, 11 I c, 13 I, II
data processing 19
decisional
— analyses 10 V
— leeway, see interpretive leeway
definitions (legal) 6 b, 9 I
democratic legitimacy and legal
 application, see Representation,
 notion of
dialectic of norm and matter 14 c,
 16 II
discretion 17
distinguishing 12 I a
double effect in the law 5 I
effectiveness of legal norms, see
 chance of enforcement
effectiveness, see likelihood of
 enforcement
elements (statutory), elements of
 the case 5, 6, 16 I
equity, see also justice in the individual case 11 I c
equivalence of construction 3 I b
establishment of facts
— judicial 15 II, III, 16 III

— in the administration 16 III
evaluation principle 15 III b
exact legal language 18, 19 b
exceptions to the general (legal) rule 7
— as a gap problem 11 I b, II b, 12 I c
experimenting thinking 12 I
extensional conceptual formation 12 I c
factual question 15
fictions 6 c
finding the applicable law (norm) 14
formalism 11 I c
functionality, requirement of
— interpretation 3 I b, 10 I
— discretion (exercise of) 17 b
— law 3 I b, 11 I b
gaps in the law 3 I b, 11, 12 I, 18 II c
general legal principles, see legal
 principles
grammatical interpretation 8, 9 II a
guaranteed law, see likelihood of enforcement
hermeneutic circle; see also interactions 10 IV
historical interpretation 8, 10 II
historical legal school 4 II b, 8, 13 I
history of creation, see historical interpretation
indeterminacy of legal concepts, see
 interpretive leeway, range of
 meaning
individual case justice 9 II b, 18 II a
inquisition maxim 15 III b
interactions, hermeneutic 3 I c, 10
 III, IV, 14 II, 16 II
interpretation
— living 4 III
— and gap-filling 9 II, 12 I
— problem-oriented 10 II
— "subjective," and "objective" 4 II
— or subsumption? 16 I
interpretive
— arguments, interpretive criteria
 10, 12 II

— leeway (latitude), *see also* Range
  of Meaning 9 II, 16 II, III
— goals 4 II, 10 I
introduction of the meaning of
  words exemplarily 4 I, 9 II
is and ought 1
judge-made law 3 I a, 13
judgment leeway, *see also* leeway
  (interpretive) 16 III
"justifiable" decisions 16 III
justification reasons, *see* exceptions
  to the general (legal) rule
key concepts 3 I c, 10 III c VII
language, *see* semantics
law, objective
— a structure of prohibition 1
— as solution to questions of justice 3
— as effective regulation, *see also*
  opportunity for enforcement 2
law, subjective 1, III
leeway (room for play) in word
  meanings, *see* meaning leeway
legal
- application, *see* application
— -ethical context 3 II d, 10 III c,
  11 I c
— -consequences 5
  precision 6 b, 12 III
  factual implications 10 V
— -training 2, 11, 13
— -questions and factual questions
  15 I
— -sense, *see also* notions of justice
  3 II
— -morality, controlling, *see* notions of justice
— -principles 10 III c
— -security 3 II b, 11 I c, 12 III, 3 II
— -comparison   10 IV
legal aesthetic context 3 II d, 10 III d,
  11 I c
legal decisions: attributes of the
  draft 10 VII

legal definitions, *see* definitions
legal syllogism 16 I
legislative intent, *see* Will of the legislature
legitimacy
— of interpretation 10 I, 13 III
— of gap-filling 11 II c, 13 III
— deviation from preliminary decision 13 II
lex posterior 7 f
lex specialis 7 c
lex superior 7 e
likelihood of application, *see* likelihood of enforcement
likelihood of enforcement of the law
  2, 7 f, 13 I, IV
limiting interpretation 11 II b
logical calculus in the law 18
logical elements of interpretation 8,
  9 I, 10 III b
meaning
— range of - (with respect to legal
  words) 4 I, 9 II, 12 I, 18 II a, *see
  also* interpretive leeway (latitude)
— - change of statutes 4 III, 10 II
meaning of words 4 I
method of stating a claim or cause
  of action 6, 14 a
model cases, model types 12 I b, III
necessity as limiting the encroachment of interests 10 V, 17 b
need to supplement the law, *see*
  gaps; continued legal development
negative elements of the case 6 b
negotiation maxim 15 III b
norm area, norm program 16 II
normative theory of law 1
notions of justice, controlling 3 II, 4
  II c, 10 IV, 11 I c, 12 I b, 13 I, III,
  17 b
objectified *Geist* 4 II b
objectified regulation, law as — 4
"objective" interpretation 4 II, 10 II

open legal development 13
optimal compromise in conflicts of
interest and conflicts of principle
10 III c, V
pain and suffering table 12 III, 19 c
permission 1 III
phrasing gaps 11 I
power of judgment 14 II
practical concordance 10 III c
precedence decisions 10 IV, 12 I a,
c, III, 13 II, 17 b
preliminary decisions, binding —13
II, 17 b
prescriptive norms 1, 18 II b
prescriptive statements, command-
ments as —1 I, 18 II b
primacy of the statute 17 b
primary behavioral norms and (secondary) sanction norms 2, V 1, 14
I b
principle of proportionality 10 V, 17 b
principles 10 III c
problem solving as the task for law,
see also functionality, requirement
of 3 I
prohibition against excess 10 III c,
V, 17 b
proof, burden of —15 III
proof, rules 15 III
property as a normative concept 1
III, 5 II
pure legal doctrine 1 I
rank relationship
— between interpretation arguments 10 IV
— between norms 7 e
reasonableness 17 b
reduction 11 II b
references in the law 6 b, c
regulations and principles 10 III c
relativity of legal concepts 3 I b
representation, notion of
— and interpretation 3 II b, 4 II c,

10 II
— and exercise of discretion 17 b
restriction 11 II b
secondary norms, see primary behavioral norm
semantics 4 I, 9 II, 18
sense
— -of words 4 I
— -change of a statute 4 III, 10 II
— -context of the law 10 III
sense of the word 4 I, 9 II a
sentence 12 III, 19 c
separate treatments 7 c
social morality, see notions of justice
specialty 7 c
spirit of the law, see legal-ethical
context
standards 10 IV
state philosophy and interpretation
theory 4 II b
style of a judgment 6 a
"subjective" interpretation 4 II, 10 II
substantiation of norms 12 I c, 16 II
subsumption
— or interpretation? 16 II
— of facts under concepts of law 16 I
supplementing provisions 1 III, 6, 9 I
system
interpretation from a - 8, 10 III
legal order as axiomatic - ? 14 I, 18
systematic fairness 10 III b, c, d, 11
I b, II d
teleological
— interpretation, see statutory purpose
— reduction, quod vide
timely interpretation 4 III
topic14 I a
trial requirements 14 I b
type 4 I
understanding 4 I
unity of the law, see also legal system 10 I

validity of the law, *see also* likelihood of enforcement 2
valuable experience 3 II
valuation concepts, *see also* general
  clauses 4 I, 9 II, 16 II
valuation inconsistencies 10 III c
valuations 3 II, 10, 11, 12 Ib, 17
—in the legal order, *see* legal aesthetic context
—and concretization 16 II
"verbal starting basis" for interpretation 8, 9
Volksgeist 4 II b, 8
will of the legislature 4 II, 8, 10 II
words as symbols 4 I